P9-BBT-690

cooking with kids

Linda Collister

photography by **Vanessa Davies**

cooking with kids

RYLAND
PETERS
& SMALL
LONDON NEW YORK

Designer Catherine Griffin
Commissioning Editor Elsa Petersen-Schepelern
Editor Susan Stuck
Production Deborah Werner
Art Director Gabriella Le Grazie
Publishing Director Alison Starling

Food Stylist Lucy McKelvie
Stylist Helen Trent
Indexer Hilary Bird

With love and thanks to my lovely, greedy kids

First published in the USA in 2003
Ryland Peters & Small, Inc.
519 Broadway, 5th Floor
New York, NY 10012
www.rylandpeters.com

10 9 8 7 6 5 4 3

Text © Linda Collister 2003
Design and photographs
© Ryland Peters & Small 2003

Printed in China

Library of Congress Cataloging-in-Publication Data

Collister, Linda.

  Cooking with kids / Linda Collister ; photography by Vanessa Davies.

    p. cm.

  Includes index.

  ISBN 1-84172-498-X

  1. Cookery. I. Title.

TX652.C7135 2003

641.5'123–dc21

          2003005188

Author's acknowledgments
I would like to thank the following for their help with this book: Elsa Petersen-Schepelern, Catherine Griffin, Susan Stuck, Vanessa Davies, Lucie McKelvie, Helen Trent, Barbara Levy, Daniel, Stevie, Emily, and Alan Hertz, Emi Kazuko, Elaine Hallgarten, Alyson Cook, Michelle Kershaw and Lakeland Ltd, Simon Silverwood and Alan Silverwood Ltd, the children and staff of Darell School, Eve De Leon Allen, Emma Greenwood, Scarlett Honey McKelvie, Algernon and Stanley Mitchell, Susannah and Olivia Nettleton, and Julia Niedertubbesing-Lopez.

Notes
• All spoon measurements are level unless otherwise specified.
• All eggs are large, unless otherwise specified. Uncooked or partially cooked eggs should not be served to the very young, the very old, those with compromised immune systems, or to pregnant women.
• Before baking, weigh or measure all ingredients exactly and prepare baking pans or sheets.

contents

just for fun ...	6
little snacks	8
light suppers	30
baking afternoon	58
real meals	82
lunchboxes	112
websites and mail order	126
conversion charts	126
index	127

just for fun ...

I'm lucky—I have been surrounded by good food for as long as I can remember. My parents loved to travel and eat out, and saw no reason not to share that with us.

I didn't set out to teach my own children how to cook—they just joined in. Like my own parents, I could see no reason to stop them. I still can't.

Cooking as a family activity started when Emily was 18 months old. She sat in a corner of the kitchen, away from the business end, stirring a bowl of batter. Then from the majesty of her highchair she watched, agog, as pancakes sizzled on the griddle. Finally she got to eat the stack she had made, sticky with peanut butter and maple syrup! Now every Sunday begins with pancakes. All three children measure, beat, fold in egg whites, cook, flip, and serve—they even set the table.

Planning meals and shopping for them are important, too. From watching and listening to my (admittedly fussy) mother-in-law at the butcher's, Daniel learned how to choose between different cuts of meat. When Stevie was going through her Think Pink stage at three, she planned all-pink meals. Her masterpiece was a warm salad of fresh borlotti beans, fresh cherries, and grilled duck breasts with a raspberry vinaigrette. She got the idea looking around the local Italian fruit and vegetable market.

So how do you get children involved? Start by picking a recipe or a menu together, then shopping together, paying careful attention to the ingredients. With very young children, try choosing fruit for a salad and asking which should be peeled, which have seeds, which don't need cutting up. Talk about where the fruits come from and why they are good for you.

In the kitchen, of course, you need some ground rules. These are just common sense, but they must be stated clearly and explained. Wash your hands, pull up long sleeves, tie back long hair, wear an apron. Make sure they understand that kitchen knives and other equipment are not toys, but can harm if not treated carefully, and that the stove can get very hot, so they should keep their distance.

Read the recipe through with the child before you start, so you both know what you are doing. Then get out all the equipment and ingredients. If possible, invest in a few pieces of child-friendly, good-quality equipment (not those kiddy-cooking packs from toy shops). Ideally, children should have their own vegetable peeler and vegetable knife with handles they can grip easily. A nonstick skillet (not too heavy), nonstick baking and roasting pans, bowls with non-slip rubber bases, a rotary cheese-grater and rotary or electric mixer, plus a kitchen timer are all useful—and don't forget good oven mitts.

Decide which parts of the recipe your children can safely manage—you know their abilities best—then work together. Older children with cooking experience can usually get a cake in and out of the oven (remind them to use oven mitts), but straining a saucepan full of boiling pasta or vegetables is best done by an adult. Obviously, never leave a child alone in the kitchen while you are both cooking, and warn them not to make secret meals and snacks (though I'm sure I'm not the only mom who's been served an interesting breakfast in bed on Mother's Day).

I'm hoping that when my children finish grade school they can make, and enjoy, a good healthy meal for themselves. It would also be nice if they could use the washing machine, the vacuum cleaner, the garden rake, and the duster—not just the computer.

little snacks

Children always arrive home from school starving, and need something to keep them going until supper appears—so these are ideas for them to make when they have to eat right away! Sliced bread can quickly be turned into cinnamon toast (just buttered toast plus sugar and spice) or a filling grilled cheese sandwich. Some snacks will keep, happily waiting for them— hummus (a creamy, soft vegetarian pâté made with chickpeas) can be stored in the refrigerator overnight, and homemade frozen treats can stay in the freezer for a couple of weeks. No time at all? Then make a fruit smoothie in the blender.

The quickest treat yet invented—hot buttered toast sprinkled with cinnamon-flavored sugar, then broiled until crunchy. Thick slices of bread, challah, or brioche (two kinds of soft bread) work best, but you can also choose bagels or English muffins split in half.

cinnamon toast

1 ASK AN ADULT to preheat the broiler.

2 Toast the 2 slices of bread in a toaster. Carefully remove the hot toast from the toaster, then spread it with butter, using as much or as little as you like.

3 Mix the sugar with the cinnamon, then sprinkle over the buttered toast to cover in an even layer. You could also put the mixture in an old sugar shaker, carefully screw on the top, then shake it over the toast.

4 ASK AN ADULT TO HELP YOU put the toast under the broiler for 30 seconds to 1 minute until the sugar has melted and looks all bubbly, then carefully remove it.

5 Let cool for a minute (the sugar is very hot and will burn your lips) before eating.

2 thick slices of bread

unsalted butter

1½ tablespoons sugar

½ teaspoon ground cinnamon

SERVES 1 OR 2

This is the traditional way to make grilled cheese—in a nonstick or electric skillet. It makes the best, crunchiest, runniest sandwiches. You can also use whatever filling you like.

grilled cheese sandwich

softened butter, for spreading

2 thick slices of bread

a slice of Cheddar or Swiss cheese (about 2 oz.)

SERVES 1

1 Butter one side of each piece of bread. Put the cheese on the unbuttered side of 1 piece of the bread, then cover with the second piece so the buttered side faces up (the reverse of a regular cheese sandwich).

2 ASK AN ADULT TO HELP YOU heat the skillet to medium for a couple of minutes, then carefully put the sandwich into the skillet. The butter will start sizzling straight away. Cook for 2 to 3 minutes until the underside is golden brown, then carefully turn the sandwich over with a spatula. Cook the second side in the same way for 2 to 3 minutes.

3 Carefully lift the sandwich out of the pan and onto a plate. Cut in half, then eat.

Other ideas
• Add a slice of ham to the cheese filling, rather like a Croque Monsieur in France.
• Add 2 or 3 slices of tomato or large mushroom.

Use your favorite hard cheese, such as Cheddar or Swiss, then add extra ingredients as you fancy.

cheese melts

3 oz. cheese

½ teaspoon Dijon or mild mustard

a big pinch of freshly ground black pepper

1 teaspoon softened butter

MAKES 2 THICK SLICES

1 ASK AN ADULT TO HELP YOU heat the broiler to its highest setting.

2 Toast the bread on both sides under the broiler or in a toaster.

3 While the bread is toasting, grate the cheese with a rotary grater (or ordinary kitchen grater) into a small bowl.

4 Put the mustard, pepper, and butter in the bowl and mix well with a small spatula or a table knife.

5 Divide the cheese mixture in half, then spread one half on each slice of toast (if you want to make only one piece of cheese melt, cover the rest of the cheese mixture and keep in the refrigerator for up to 4 days).

6 Carefully put the cheese-covered toast under the hot broiler and leave for 1 to 2 minutes until golden brown and bubbly. When cheese melts, its fats become very hot and can easily burn, so take great care as you lift it out of the broiler, and ASK AN ADULT TO HELP. Let cool for a minute before eating.

Other ideas
- Put a slice of ham on top of the toast, spread with the cheese mixture, then broil.
- Spread about 1 tablespoon canned tuna (well-drained) over the toast, cover with the cheese mix, then broil (don't worry if it gets a bit mixed up).
- Put about 3 slices of tomato on top of the cheese mix on the toast before broiling.

This fruity salsa is delicious with Cheese Melts and also with Tortilla Chips (page 19).

fresh peach salsa

1 large ripe peach

3 cherry tomatoes

1 small lime

a few fresh cilantro leaves or chives

a big pinch of hot red pepper flakes

salt and freshly ground black pepper

SERVES 1 OR 2

1 Using a small sharp knife, slice the peach in half from top to bottom. Twist the halves in opposite directions, then pull apart. Ease out the pit. Turn the peach halves flat side down on a chopping board and cut into small cubes. Put the pieces in a small bowl.

2 Cut each tomato in 4 and add to the bowl.

3 Cut the lime in half and squeeze out the juice with a lemon squeezer. Pour it over the peach and tomato pieces. Using kitchen shears, snip the cilantro or chives into the bowl. Add the pepper flakes, salt, and pepper and mix well with a small spoon. Taste, and add more pepper flakes, salt, or pepper as needed.

4 Eat immediately or cover and keep in the refrigerator for up to 4 hours.

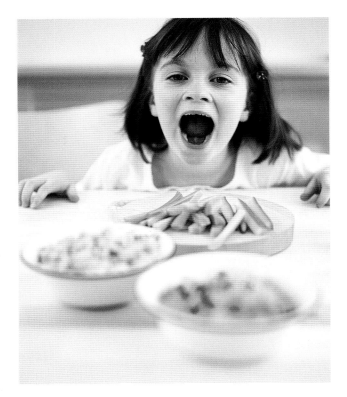

hummus

15 oz. canned chickpeas, about 2 cups

2 tablespoons tahini paste

2 tablespoons olive oil

1 lemon

1 garlic clove

a small handful of parsley leaves

a big pinch of salt

a big pinch of ground black pepper

a big pinch of ground cumin

sweet paprika, for sprinkling

SERVES 4 TO 6

Hummus is good for spreading on toast or warm pita breads, and also as a dip for carrot, cucumber, and celery sticks. This recipe makes a slightly crunchy spread.

1 Carefully open the can of chickpeas. Put a colander in the (empty) sink, drain the chickpeas into the colander, then rinse them under cold running water. Shake the colander well to drain off the water. Take out 1 heaping tablespoon of chickpeas and save to add at the end.

2 Tip the rest of the chickpeas into a food processor—ASK AN ADULT TO HELP whenever you use it. Add the tahini and olive oil.

3 Cut the lemon in half and squeeze out the juice with a lemon squeezer. Peel the garlic. Rinse the parsley. Put the lemon juice, garlic, parsley, salt, pepper, and cumin in the food processor.

4 Run the processor for about 20 seconds, then turn it off. Scrape down the sides with a plastic spatula, then process again for about 10 seconds to make a fairly smooth purée. Add the saved whole chickpeas and process (using the pulse button if possible) for 3 to 4 seconds.

5 ASK AN ADULT to remove the sharp blade from the food processor. Spoon the hummus into a serving dish and pat down the surface until it is smooth. Sprinkle the top with a little paprika, then serve.

6 The hummus can be kept, well covered, in the refrigerator for up to 1 week.

Eat with tortilla chips (recipe below), spread on toast, or with raw vegetable sticks. Use a small serrated knife for cutting up the tomato. Ask an adult to help you if you haven't used a sharp knife before.

guacamole

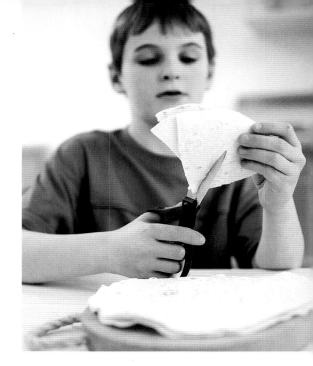

1 large, very ripe avocado

1 large or 2 small tomatoes

1 lime

1 small garlic clove

a big pinch of salt

a big pinch of freshly ground black pepper

SERVES 2 TO 4

1 Using a small, sharp knife, cut the avocado in half all around from top to bottom. Twist the fruit gently and pull the two halves away from each other. Using a teaspoon, scoop out the flesh from each half into a small bowl, and throw away the seed and skin. Gently mash the flesh with a fork to make a lumpy purée.

2 Rinse the tomato, then cut into quarters on a chopping board. Cut away the small green core at the top of the tomato, then chop each quarter into about 6 pieces. Add to the bowl. Cut the lime in half, then squeeze out the juice with a lemon squeezer. Add 2 teaspoons of the juice to the bowl, but keep the rest in case you need to add it later.

3 Peel the garlic and crush it with a garlic press or chop it very finely. Add to the bowl, then add the salt and pepper. Mix all the ingredients together with the fork—the mixture should be a bit lumpy. Taste and add more lime juice or salt and pepper as needed.

4 Eat immediately with these home-baked tortilla chips.

Turn ready-made soft wheat tortillas into a crunchy snack by baking them in the oven.

home-baked tortilla chips

4 large or 6 medium wheat flour tortillas

a large baking sheet

SERVES 4 TO 6

1 ASK AN ADULT TO HELP YOU heat the oven to 325°F. Using kitchen shears, cut each tortilla into 8 wedges. Spread the wedges in one layer, not overlapping, on the baking sheet.

2 ASK AN ADULT TO HELP YOU bake them in the oven—they will need 15 minutes until they turn crisp and dry. Carefully remove the baking sheet from the oven. Eat while still warm or let cool first.

2 large unwaxed lemons

⅓ cup sugar

6 oz. fresh or frozen raspberries, about 1 cup

1 cup cold water

2 cups sparkling water

12 ice cubes

a blender

MAKES 4 GLASSES

With an adult to help with slicing, even quite small children can make this recipe. You'll need a blender, fresh unwaxed lemons, plus raspberries (or strawberries) for this fizzy, refreshing, healthy cool drink.

fresh raspberry lemonade

1 Rinse the lemons, because you will be using the skin as well as the juice.

2 Carefully cut each lemon into 8 with a small kitchen knife— ASK AN ADULT TO HELP YOU if you haven't used a kitchen knife before.

3 Put the lemons, sugar, raspberries, and the 1 cup cold water in a blender. Make sure the lid is on tight, then blend for 10 seconds.

4 When the machine has stopped, remove the lid—check to see that the lemon pieces are about the size of peas. If there are still large pieces, blend again for 5 seconds. Remove the blender pitcher from the machine.

5 Put a medium strainer on top of a large serving pitcher. Carefully pour the lemon mixture into the pitcher through the strainer. Using a spoon, gently press down on the lemons to squeeze out all the juice. Throw away the lemon pieces.

6 Top up the juice with the sparkling water—it will foam up, so add it slowly. Stir in the ice cubes and serve in chilled glasses.

Not a package mix but the real thing—real chocolate, milk, and a dash of sugar, plus whipped cream and mini marshmallows if you really want to have fun.

real hot chocolate

1 Put the chocolate, sugar, and milk in a small saucepan. ASK AN ADULT TO HELP YOU heat up the milk until it is almost boiling. Stir occasionally with a wooden spoon to help the chocolate melt.

2 Remove the saucepan from the heat and put onto a heatproof surface.

3 Using a rotary beater, beat the mixture until it is very smooth and foaming.

4 Carefully pour the hot chocolate into a mug and serve.

Other ideas
• Top with a swirl of cream (from a can, or whip some cream in a bowl with the rotary beater). Sprinkle with a few mini marshmallows, then serve.

1½ oz. bittersweet chocolate

1 teaspoon sugar

⅔ cup milk

To serve (optional)

whipped cream

mini marshmallows

SERVES 1

**Perfect on a really hot day when you want
a filling drink, but not a milkshake.**

mango smoothie

1 cup fresh or
frozen mango
pieces

1 ripe banana

1 cup chilled fresh
orange juice

ice cubes
(optional)

SERVES 2

1 Put the mango pieces into a large blender or food processor.

2 Peel off the banana skin, then slice up the banana and put the slices in the blender too. Pour in the orange juice. Put on the lid and secure tightly—ASK AN ADULT TO HELP YOU blend the mixture until completely smooth and foamy.

3 Pour into tall glasses and add ice cubes and a straw if you like.

Note If you chill the glasses in the refrigerator first (not the freezer), you get a lovely frosty effect.

**This is a simple fruit and milk recipe—you can add a
scoop of strawberry ice cream or sorbet if you like.**

strawberry milkshake

1 pint ripe
strawberries

1 ripe banana

¾ cup chilled milk

SERVES 2

1 Wipe the strawberries with paper towels, then carefully pull out the leafy green tops. ASK AN ADULT TO HELP YOU put the strawberries in the blender or food processor.

2 Peel the banana and cut it into slices. Put them into the blender, then add the cold milk.

3 Put on the lid and secure tightly—ASK AN ADULT TO HELP YOU blend the mixture until smooth and foaming.

4 Pour into chilled glasses and drink.

These are very popular in fancy ice cream parlors in New England. You can use your favorite chocolate—milk, white, or bittersweet, or even layer them for a striped finish.

chocolate bananas

1 banana per person

1½ oz. chocolate per banana

To decorate

chopped nuts or grated coconut

small bamboo skewers

SERVES 1

1 Peel the banana and cut it into pieces about 1 inch long. Carefully push a short skewer up through the center of each piece. Wrap in plastic, then freeze for at least 2 hours or overnight.

2 When ready to eat, carefully and gently melt the chocolate in the microwave or in a small heatproof bowl set over a small saucepan of steaming hot water—ASK AN ADULT TO HELP YOU do this. It will take 15 seconds in the microwave or about 1 to 2 minutes over a saucepan.

3 Unwrap the banana pieces. Hold one piece by the stick over the bowl of chocolate, then spoon the chocolate over the banana to coat it.

4 The chocolate will set very quickly, so if you want to decorate it, sprinkle with chopped nuts or grated coconut as soon as you have coated the banana. You can add a second layer of chocolate in a contrasting color.

5 Eat immediately.

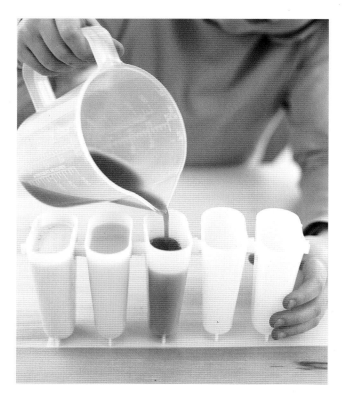

**1¾–3 cups fruit yogurt,
or fresh fruit juice**

a frozen treat maker

MAKES 8 TREATS

You can buy inexpensive plastic frozen-treat kits in supermarkets and kitchen stores, and also by mail order. They usually make about 8 treats at one time and fit easily onto a freezer shelf.

frozen treats

1 Each treat will use ¼ to ⅓ cup liquid. Using a teaspoon, carefully spoon the yogurt into the treat molds, filling them almost to the top—the mixture will expand when it's frozen, so don't fill the molds to the top. If using fruit juice, put it in a small pitcher and pour it carefully into the molds.

2 Gently bang the molds on the work surface 2 or 3 times to get rid of any large air bubbles (otherwise your frozen treats will have holes in them).

3 Carefully push the handle tops into each treat. Put the container into the freezer on a flat shelf—don't balance it on something else or you may end up with funny-shaped treats. Freeze until solid—at least 4 hours or overnight.

4 To remove the treats from the container, stand the container in a bowl of cold water (or hold it under cold running water) for 1 to 2 minutes until the treats lift out of the container.

Other ideas
• If you use fruit juice, shake the juice container carefully to mix the contents, then pour it into the treat container and freeze as before.
• You can also freeze the recipes for Mango Smoothie and Strawberry Milkshake (page 25).

A quick snack is one thing, but this is real cooking. These recipes are fairly quick, but need a bit of parental help with the dangerously hot bits. I've never met a child who doesn't like pasta, and simple fresh sauces are easily made. Daniel was given an inexpensive pasta machine for Christmas and when he has a friend over for supper, they would rather make their own pasta than watch television. It takes about 30 minutes to make pasta. For each serving allow 1 large egg and ¾ cup all-purpose flour. Mix the dough in a food processor, knead it, then roll and cut in the pasta machine following the manufacturer's instructions.

light suppers

This simple tomato sauce is perfect with pasta—and because there's no cooking, it's quick too.

fresh tomato sauce with pasta

1 lb. ripe tomatoes

a small bunch of fresh chives

a small handful of fresh basil leaves

1 garlic clove

¼ cup virgin olive oil

a pinch of salt

a pinch of freshly ground black pepper

To serve

14 oz. spaghetti

freshly grated Parmesan cheese

SERVES 4

1 Rinse the tomatoes and put them on a chopping board. Cut each tomato into quarters, then cut each quarter into about 4 chunks. Have a large heatproof serving bowl ready and put the cut tomatoes straight in the bowl. Using kitchen shears, snip the chives into tiny lengths straight into the bowl. Tear the basil leaves and add to the bowl.

2 Peel the garlic and crush with a garlic press or chop finely and add to the bowl. Add the olive oil, salt, and pepper. Stir thoroughly. Taste the sauce—it may need more salt and pepper, a pinch of sugar, or even a squeeze of lemon juice, depending on the flavor of the tomatoes. Let the sauce stand while you cook the pasta—or for up to an hour—for the flavors to develop. If possible, cover the bowl and put it in the sun.

3 ASK AN ADULT TO HELP YOU cook the spaghetti in a large saucepan of boiling water with a pinch of salt. Let it cook for 8 to 10 minutes or follow the instructions on the package. Drain carefully, then add the pasta to the sauce. Toss gently until well mixed, then serve with plenty of freshly grated Parmesan cheese.

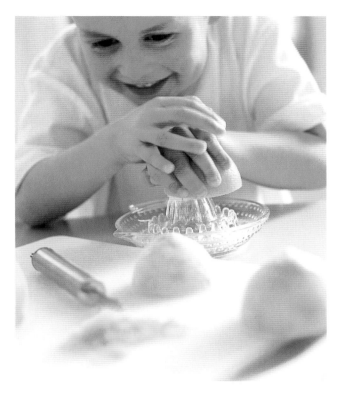

A simple and fast pasta dish that's good on its own or with cooked chicken (see Italian Roast Chicken page 87). While the pasta is cooking, you make the lemon and watercress dressing in the serving bowl.

zingy pasta

1 large unwaxed lemon

¼ cup light cream

1 tablespoon unsalted butter, at room temperature

1 cup watercress sprigs, rinsed

3 good pinches of salt

freshly ground black pepper

8 oz. thin dried egg pasta, such as tagliolini

1 cup freshly grated Parmesan cheese, to serve

SERVES 4

1 ASK AN ADULT to fill a large saucepan with water, add a pinch of salt, and put it on the stove to boil.

2 While the water is heating, rinse the lemon, then grate the yellow part of the peel into a large heatproof serving bowl—leave the white part on the fruit because it is bitter. You can grate with the fine-hole side of a grater or with a hand-held lemon zester which removes the zest in thin strips. Cut the lemon in half and squeeze out the juice with a lemon squeezer. Pour the juice into the serving bowl.

3 Add the cream, butter, watercress sprigs, and remaining salt to the bowl, then add about 4 turns of the pepper grinder.

4 When the water boils, ASK AN ADULT TO HELP YOU add the pasta to the water and stir. Using a timer or clock, cook for 2 to 3 minutes or according to the package instructions—pasta tastes best when it is not overcooked. ASK AN ADULT to drain the pasta and add it to the bowl. The heat of the pasta will warm the ingredients and wilt the watercress.

5 Hold a fork in each hand and carefully lift and toss the pasta several times so it is thoroughly coated in the sauce. Eat immediately sprinkled with Parmesan.

Strips of smoked salmon turn this creamy pasta sauce a pretty pink. My daughter called it after her favorite doll. For a stronger flavor, add snipped fresh chives or dill.

pink dolly's pasta

10 oz. egg fettuccine

4 oz. smoked salmon or smoked trout (trimmings are fine)

¼ cup heavy cream

black pepper

a small bunch fresh chives or a few sprigs of dill

SERVES 4

1 To make the sauce, snip the smoked salmon into small strips (you don't have to do this with trimmings) and put in a small saucepan. Add the cream and about 3 grinds of pepper from the pepper mill.

2 ASK AN ADULT TO HELP YOU set the saucepan over the lowest possible heat and warm the ingredients so the cream melts and the salmon turns a pale pink. Turn off the heat under the pan.

3 Cook the pasta in boiling salted water following the recipe on page 35. Allow 4 to 6 minutes cooking time, or follow the package instructions.

4 When the pasta is just tender and ready to be drained, ASK AN ADULT to remove about half a ladle (about ¼ cup) of water from the pasta pan and add it to the small pan with the sauce. Drain the pasta into a colander.

5 Tip the pasta into a large serving bowl and pour the sauce over the top. Hold a fork in each hand and carefully lift and toss the pasta until well mixed. Using kitchen shears, snip the chives or dill straight onto the pasta. Then serve with salad or green vegetables.

Another idea
• Add 1 cup frozen peas or corn to the sauce before you add the pepper.

We call this red, green, and white salad "Flag Salad" because it has the same colors as the flag of Italy. Use your fingers to pull the mozzarella apart into stringy pieces, tear up the basil and salad leaves, then scoop out the avocados with a teaspoon. Salad dressings are easy to make too—just put all the ingredients in a screw-top jar and shake them.

flag salad

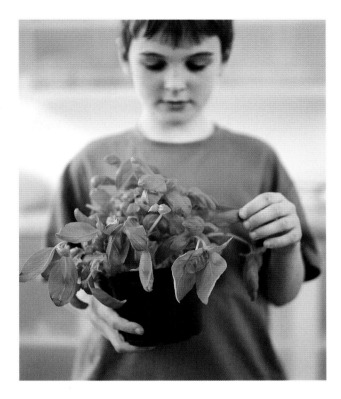

1 Thoroughly wash the salad leaves in a bowl of cold water. Drain well, then spin-dry in a salad spinner or pat dry with paper towels. Tear any large leaves in half (discard any brown parts) and arrange on a large serving platter.

2 Wash the tomatoes. Very small cherry tomatoes can be left whole, but cut larger ones in half on a chopping board with a small serrated knife. If you haven't used a serrated knife before, ASK AN ADULT TO HELP YOU. Dot the tomatoes over the salad leaves.

3 Slice the avocados in half from top to bottom, then twist the avocados to separate the halves and pull apart. Use a teaspoon to scoop out the flesh in spoon-shaped pieces, straight onto the salad. Discard the big seeds and skins.

4 Open the bag or container of mozzarella over the sink and drain off the watery white liquid. Using your hands, pull the mozzarella into shreds and arrange on top of the salad.

5 Rinse the basil leaves, then tear them up into big pieces and add to the salad.

6 To make the dressing, put all the dressing ingredients in a small screw-top jar. Fasten the lid securely, then shake the jar until the dressing looks creamy—this is called "emulsified." Open the jar and taste the dressing—add more salt or pepper as needed.

7 Pour the dressing in a thin stream over the top of the salad and eat it immediately.

1 cup arugula leaves or watercress sprigs or 1 small lettuce

1 cup cherry tomatoes, about 25

2 ripe avocados

12 oz. fresh mozzarella cheese

a handful of basil leaves

Dressing

2 tablespoons virgin olive oil

2 tablespoons balsamic vinegar

a big pinch of salt

a big pinch of freshly ground black pepper

¼ teaspoon honey

**SERVES 4 AS AN ENTRÉE:
6 AS AN APPETIZER**

You can make your own pizza from scratch in half an hour. You can add anything you like as a topping – though this mixture is always popular.

easy speedy pizza

1 ASK AN ADULT TO HELP YOU preheat the oven to 400°F. Grease 2 large baking sheets with a little soft butter on a paper towel.

2 Set a sieve over a large bowl. Tip the flour, sugar, baking soda, and salt into the sieve and sift it into the bowl. Stir in the dried herbs.

3 Using your hand, make a hollow in the middle of the flour and pour in the buttermilk or the yogurt and milk mixture. Using one hand, start to mix the flour into the liquid, then gradually work all the flour into the dough to make a soft and slightly sticky mixture. If there are dry crumbs and it is hard to work all the flour into the dough, add 1 tablespoon of buttermilk or milk. However, if the dough is really sticky and feels very wet, work in more flour, 1 tablespoon at a time.

4 When the dough comes together in a ball, tip it out of the bowl onto a work surface lightly sprinkled with flour. Work the ball of dough with both hands for 1 minute until it looks smooth.

5 Divide the dough into 4 equal pieces—use a round-bladed knife. Shape each piece into a neat ball. Flour your hands, then gently pat out each piece of the dough to a round about 7 inches across. Set the rounds slightly apart on the baking sheets.

6 Wash your hands, then wipe down the work surface to make it easier to prepare the topping.

7 ASK AN ADULT TO HELP YOU open the can of tomatoes. Set a large sieve over a bowl, then tip the can of tomatoes into the sieve and let them drain for a couple of minutes.

Pizza base

3 cups all-purpose flour

1 teaspoon sugar

1 teaspoon baking soda

1 teaspoon salt

½ teaspoon dried oregano or thyme

1½ cups buttermilk or ¾ cup plain yogurt plus ¾ cup milk

butter, for greasing

Cheese and tomato topping

14 oz. canned chopped tomatoes, 2 cups

1 tablespoon tomato paste

1 tablespoon olive oil

1 teaspoon dried oregano or thyme

a pinch of salt

a pinch of freshly ground black pepper

1 garlic clove

12 oz. fresh mozzarella cheese

Optional extras

green or black pitted olives, slices of pepperoni or ham, sliced red or green pepper, or mushrooms

2 large baking sheets

MAKES 4 MEDIUM PIZZAS

8 Pour the tomatoes into a food processor or blender (the juice drained off can be saved for soups or sauces). Add the tomato paste, olive oil, herbs, salt, and pepper to the processor. Peel the garlic and add it too. Don't forget to put on the lid! ASK AN ADULT TO HELP YOU blend the tomato mixture very briefly just to make a lumpy purée. Tip the mixture into a bowl.

9 Spoon 2 tablespoons of the tomato topping in the middle of each pizza. Spread the tomato mixture over the base leaving a 1-inch border of uncovered dough all around the edge.

10 Slice the mozzarella or pull it into long shreds. Arrange the pieces on top of the pizza.

11 Finally, top with as many extras as you like.

12 ASK AN ADULT TO HELP YOU bake the pizzas until they are a light golden brown and bubbling—this takes 15 to 18 minutes in the preheated oven.

13 Carefully remove from the oven, but let cool for a couple of minutes before eating—the melted cheese can burn your mouth.

Making a risotto is simple, but the special arborio rice does need constant stirring as it cooks. You can pick fresh peas from the garden or farmers' market, or use frozen peas.

pea and parmesan risotto

1 medium onion

2 garlic cloves

2 tablespoons virgin olive oil

1⅓ cups Italian arborio rice

1¼ cups shelled fresh or frozen peas

about 3 cups hot vegetable stock

1 tablespoon unsalted butter

salt and freshly ground black pepper

1 cup freshly grated Parmesan cheese

a few sprigs of parsley

SERVES 4

1 Peel the onion and garlic, then chop them finely—ASK AN ADULT TO HELP YOU do this in a food processor or on a chopping board, using a small kitchen knife.

2 Put the olive oil in a medium, heavy saucepan.

3 Put the pan over very low heat and stir in the chopped vegetables. Cook gently for about 10 minutes so the onion turns clear and not brown. Stir in the rice, then stir in the peas.

4 Turn up the heat to medium and add a ladle of the hot vegetable stock. Stir gently so it doesn't splash you, and as soon as the liquid is absorbed by the rice, add another ladle of stock.

5 Keep on stirring the rice very gently the whole time so it doesn't stick to the bottom or sides of the pan, and keep on adding the hot stock. It will take about 20 minutes of stirring before the rice is tender. Taste a few grains with a teaspoon, but let it cool first so you don't burn your mouth. The mixture should be creamy and moist, but not dry or very wet and soupy—the exact amount of stock you will need depends on the brand of rice you use and how fast the rice is cooking.

6 As soon as the rice is tender, turn off the heat. Add the butter, salt, and pepper, plus half the grated cheese. Stir gently into the rice, then cover the pan and leave for 4 to 5 minutes.

7 Rinse the parsley sprigs and snip them with kitchen shears. Uncover the pan, sprinkle the parsley on top, then serve immediately with the extra grated cheese.

No cooking needed here—slices of smoked salmon or smoked trout are arranged in Belgian endive leaf "boats," then topped with a tangy cream dressing. For a special meal, serve the boats with whole wheat bread, such as the Grant Loaf (page 81). The palest leaves will be the sweetest—don't use green ones.

smoked salmon in endive "boats"

1 Gently separate the lettuce leaves and wash them in plenty of cold water. Drain thoroughly in a colander, discard any brown or bruised leaves, then spin dry in a salad spinner or pat dry with paper towels.

2 Tear up any large leaves, then arrange the leaves on a large plate.

3 Using a small sharp knife, carefully cut off the stalk end of each head of endive.

4 Gently peel off the leaves—take care not to tear them. Wash and dry the endive leaves in the same way as the lettuce.

5 Choose the 16 largest and best leaves—save the rest to make another salad.

6 To make up the "boats," set the endive leaves, without overlapping, on top of the lettuce on the platter.

7 Using kitchen shears, carefully cut the slices of smoked salmon or trout into 16 strips to fit inside the endive "boats." Carefully arrange the fish in the endive "boats."

8 To make the dressing, put the sour cream, lemon juice, salt, black pepper, and cayenne pepper in a small bowl. Snip the fresh herbs into small pieces with kitchen shears and add to the bowl. Stir gently, then taste—add more lemon juice, salt, or pepper as needed.

9 Using a teaspoon, put a blob of the dressing in each endive "boat," then serve.

1 small crisp lettuce, such as romaine heart, or a package of salad leaves

2 medium heads of Belgian endive (total weight about 6 oz.)

4 oz. smoked salmon, smoked trout, ham, or smoked turkey

Herb dressing

3 tablespoons sour cream

a squeeze of lemon juice

a big pinch of salt

a big pinch of freshly ground black pepper

a big pinch of cayenne pepper

1 tablespoon fresh dill leaves, parsley sprigs, or a small bunch of chives

SERVES 4

Sushi is a famous rice dish from Japan. There are many kinds, but one of the most delicious is a roll made of seaweed, rice, and cucumber, rolled up, then cut into bite-size pieces. Dip them in soy sauce before eating. Another easy kind is made in an egg cup—just smoked salmon and rice, all wrapped up.

two kinds of sushi

1¾ cups Japanese sushi rice

Vinegar dressing
3 tablespoons Japanese rice vinegar
2½ tablespoons sugar
2 teaspoons salt

Hand vinegar
¼ cup Japanese rice vinegar
1 cup cold water

Egg cup sushi
4 oz. smoked salmon slices

Sushi rolls
1 medium cucumber, about 8 inches
3 sheets nori seaweed

To serve
Japanese soy sauce
pickled ginger (optional)

sushi mat or clingfilm

MAKES 10 EGG CUPS AND 36 ROLLS

Cooking the rice

1 To prepare the sushi rice, measure the rice in a measuring cup. Put a large bowl in the sink, add the rice, then cover with water from the cold tap. Swish your hand about in the rice to wash the grains, then carefully tip off the water without tipping out any of the rice. Do this once more, then add enough cold water to cover the rice well, and let soak for 10 minutes.

2 Drain off the water, then drain the rice into a colander set over the sink.

3 Transfer the rice to a deep, heavy saucepan, and pour in 1¾ cups cold water. Cover the pan. ASK AN ADULT TO HELP YOU cook the rice. Bring the rice to a boil over high heat—this will take about 5 minutes.

4 Turn down the heat so it is quite low and let simmer without lifting the lid for 10 minutes, so that it's all absorbed. Turn off the heat and leave it, still without lifting the lid, for 10 to 15 minutes.

Making the vinegar dressing and hand vinegar

1 While the rice is cooking, make the vinegar dressing for the rice. Put the rice vinegar, sugar, and salt in a small bowl, then stir well until dissolved.

2 To make the hand vinegar (which stops the rice sticking to your fingers), put the vinegar and water in a bowl and stir well.

Dressing the rice with vinegar

1 Take the lid off the cooked rice. ASK AN ADULT TO HELP YOU put the hot rice into a large shallow dish. Sprinkle with the vinegar dressing. Using a wooden spatula, fold the dressing into the rice—try not to stir, and ask someone to fan the air just above the rice as you do this to help the rice cool quickly. Let cool for 5 to 10 minutes.

Making egg cup sushi

1 Using kitchen shears, cut the smoked salmon slices into 10 to 12 pieces. *continued*

sushi continued

2 Line the inside of one egg cup with a piece of plastic wrap so it hangs over the edge of the cup.

3 Line the whole of the inside of the egg cup with a piece of smoked salmon, filling in any gaps with small trimmings.

4 Dip your hands in the hand vinegar—this stops the rice from sticking to your fingers. Put about 1 tablespoon of the rice into the cup and press down gently with your thumbs. Try not to over-fill the egg cup. Fold any salmon hanging over the edge of the egg cup over the top of the rice. Lift the plastic wrap up and out of the egg cup and put the molded sushi upside down on a serving platter.

5 Repeat to make 10 pieces.

Making sushi rolls

1 Rinse the cucumber and put onto a chopping board. ASK AN ADULT TO HELP YOU cut off each end carefully with a sharp knife. Cut the cucumber in half lengthwise and scoop out the seeds with a teaspoon to make 2 "boats."

2 Cut each half cucumber lengthwise into 3 strips. Cut each sheet of seaweed in half crosswise (sometimes there is a line or crease to guide you).

3 Put the sushi mat (or you can use a sheet of plastic wrap) on the work surface and put a half-sheet of seaweed on top.

4 Dip your fingers in the hand vinegar, then take a handful of rice, 2 to 3 tablespoons, and pat it into a log shape. Then put the rice in the center of the sheet of seaweed and flatten the rice with your fingers so it covers the seaweed leaving a 1-inch margin on the far side.

5 Put 1 strip of cucumber down the middle of the rice. Pick up the mat from the side closest to you and roll the mat over to meet the other side, keeping the cucumber in the center as much as possible, and keeping the rice inside the seaweed.

6 Lift the top edge of the mat, then press and roll the mat carefully so the join in the seaweed sticks together. Lift the roll off the mat and onto a chopping board. Make 5 more rolls in the same way.

7 ASK AN ADULT TO HELP YOU cut each roll into 6 pieces. Arrange on a serving platter and serve with a dish of Japanese soy sauce for dipping, and pickled ginger slices, if you like.

Note Sushi shouldn't be put into the refrigerator because it makes the rice hard. If you are making it early for a party, keep the sushi in an airtight container in a very cool, well-shaded spot.

Pigs-in-a-blanket is a funny name for little sausages cooked in batter—funny, but delicious. Choose your favorite sausages—pork, beef, lamb, chicken, or vegetarian. You will also need thick oven mitts, because the pan gets very hot. Younger children can mix the batter, but will need an adult to do the cooking. Eat them for a winter lunch or dinner.

pigs-in-a-blanket

1 ASK AN ADULT TO HELP YOU adjust the oven shelves—you will be using the middle one for the muffin pan, so make sure there is plenty of room for the batter to rise above the pan. Put a shelf under the middle one and put a large tray or roasting pan on it to catch any drips. ASK AN ADULT TO HELP YOU preheat the oven to 425°F.

2 To make the batter, put the flour, salt, and pepper in a large bowl. Make a hollow in the center, then break the eggs into the hollow. Pour the milk into the hollow.

3 Using a wire whisk, mix the eggs with the milk. Start to mix the flour into the hollow. When all the flour has been mixed in, beat the batter well to get rid of any lumps.

4 Add the snipped chives and beat them into the batter. (The batter can be made up to 3 hours before you start cooking.)

5 Using kitchen shears, snip the links between the sausages. Wash your hands well after handling the sausages.

6 Put 1 teaspoon of oil into each hole of the muffin pan, then ASK AN ADULT TO HELP YOU put it in the oven to heat. Using thick oven mitts, remove the pan after 5 minutes—the oil will be very, very hot—and put it on a heatproof work surface. Carefully put 1 sausage in each hole, then ASK AN ADULT TO HELP YOU put the pan back in the oven for 5 minutes.

7 Pour or ladle the batter into a large measuring cup with a pouring lip, and stir it once or twice.

8 Carefully remove the hot pan as before, then stand back (the oil can splutter) and carefully pour the batter into each hole so each one is half full. Gently replace the pan in the oven and bake for 20 minutes until golden brown and crispy.

9 Remove from the oven and ease each one out of its hole with a round-bladed knife. Eat straight away with salad or green vegetables or even baked beans.

¾ cup all-purpose flour

a pinch of salt

a pinch of pepper

2 large eggs

1 cup milk

a small bunch of fresh chives (optional), snipped into 1-inch pieces with kitchen shears

12 breakfast link sausages

¼ cup vegetable oil

a large tray or roasting pan

1 or 2 large muffin pans

thick oven mitts

MAKES 12 INDIVIDUAL PIGS: SERVES 4 TO 6

You can change this basic recipe using your favorite bits and pieces from the refrigerator. The main thing is to add plenty of vegetables—the omelet is basically vegetables stuck together with eggs and cheese—though you can also add strips of ham, pepperoni, or cooked bacon, chicken, or turkey. This is easy!

spanish omelet

3 large eggs

1½ tablespoons cream (any kind)

2 tablespoons grated Cheddar cheese

a pinch of salt

a pinch of pepper

1½ tablespoons olive oil

Vegetables

2 scallions

1 medium tomato

2 tablespoons peas (cooked or frozen)

2 tablespoons corn
(cooked, frozen, or canned)

½ red or green bell pepper, or zucchini

1 cooked potato

SERVES 2

1 Break the eggs into a medium bowl. Add the cream, cheese, salt, and pepper and mix well with a fork.

2 ASK AN ADULT TO HELP YOU put the olive oil in a nonstick skillet and warm gently over low heat.

3 While the oil is heating, cut the scallions into thin slices with a small, sharp knife, and cut the tomato into small chunks.

4 Add the onion, tomato, peas, and corn to the oil and stir well with a wooden spoon. Cook gently for a few minutes while you slice the bell pepper or zucchini, and cut the potato into small cubes the size of dice. Add all these to the skillet and stir well.

5 Let cook for 2 minutes, then stir again and pour in the egg mix. Stir the whole mixture gently, then turn up the heat to medium and let cook until the eggs look almost set and no longer runny on the surface.

6 ASK AN ADULT TO HELP YOU remove the skillet from the heat and slide the omelet out of the skillet and onto a serving platter. Cut into wedges and eat.

This tomato soup is thickened with split red lentils and is packed with delicious ingredients. Serve with homemade bread, such as the Grant Loaf (page 81), for a filling meal.

tomato and red lentil soup

1 tablespoon virgin olive oil

1 medium red onion

1 medium carrot

1 celery stalk

1 garlic clove

15 oz. canned chopped tomatoes, about 2 cups

1 tablespoon tomato paste

¼ cup split red lentils

1¾ cups vegetable stock

a big pinch of salt

a big pinch of freshly ground black pepper

a big pinch of sugar

2 tablespoons cream (any kind), to serve

SERVES 4 TO 6

1 Put the oil in a medium saucepan.

2 Peel the onion, peel the carrot with a vegetable peeler, wash the celery, and peel the garlic. Using a small, sharp knife, trim off the ends of the onion, carrot, and celery, then cut them all into chunks about 1½ inches long. Put the onion, carrot, celery, and garlic in a food processor. ASK AN ADULT TO HELP YOU process the vegetables until they are very finely chopped.

3 ASK AN ADULT TO HELP YOU put the saucepan on low heat to warm the oil gently. Carefully put the vegetables into the pan. Stir gently with a wooden spoon, then cover the pan with a lid and let cook very slowly for 5 minutes. Carefully lift the lid off the pan—the steam can burn you—and add the canned tomatoes, tomato paste, red lentils, stock, salt, pepper, and sugar. Stir well, then turn up the heat so the mixture comes to a boil.

4 When the soup has boiled, cover the pan with the lid, then turn down the heat so that the soup simmers very gently. Let it cook for 30 minutes. While the soup is cooking, carefully lift the lid about every 10 minutes and stir the soup with a wooden spoon to stop the lentils sticking to the bottom of the pan and burning.

5 At the end of the cooking time, take off the lid, turn off the heat, and let the soup cool for 5 minutes.

6 ASK AN ADULT TO HELP YOU ladle the soup into a blender or food processor and blend until smooth. You can also purée the soup in the saucepan with a hand blender, but take care not to splash yourself with the hot soup. If you have used a blender or processor, tip the soup back into the saucepan. Taste—add more salt, pepper, or sugar as needed—then carefully warm up the soup over low heat (the thick soup can splutter as it comes to a boil, so stand back). As soon as it boils, turn off the heat, stir in the cream and serve.

This family favorite vegetarian soup makes a good meal on a cold day. It is full of wonderful flavors—savory, sweet, spicy, and aromatic. Ask an adult to help you if you haven't used a sharp knife before.

sweet and spicy soup

1 medium onion

2 medium potatoes

2 oz. dried apricots

½ cup split red lentils

1 lemon

3 cups vegetable stock

¼ teaspoon ground cumin

a big pinch of salt

a big pinch of freshly ground black pepper

1 teaspoon virgin olive oil or a small piece of unsalted butter, to finish

SERVES 4 TO 6

1 Peel the onion, then peel the potatoes with a vegetable peeler.

2 Using a small, sharp knife, cut the ends off the onion, then cut the onion, potatoes, and apricots into chunks.

3 Put the onions, potatoes, apricots, and lentils in a large, heavy saucepan.

4 Cut the lemon in half. Squeeze the juice from one half with a lemon squeezer (save the other half for later) and add to the pan. Pour in the stock, then add the cumin, salt, and pepper. Mix well with a wooden spoon.

5 ASK AN ADULT TO HELP YOU put the pan over medium heat and bring to a boil. Carefully stir the pan, then cover it with the lid, turn down the heat to very low so that the soup simmers very gently, and let it cook for 30 minutes. Very carefully lift off the lid and stir every 10 minutes to stop the lentils from sticking to the bottom of the pan.

6 At the end of the cooking time, turn off the heat, lift off the lid, and let the soup cool for 5 minutes.

7 ASK AN ADULT TO HELP YOU ladle the soup carefully into a blender or food processor and blend until very smooth. The soup can also be puréed in the saucepan using a hand blender, but take care because the hot soup can burn if it splashes you.

8 Pour the soup back into the pan. Taste and add more lemon juice, salt, pepper, or cumin as needed. Gently reheat the soup—be careful, because it can splutter as it comes to a boil. Turn off the heat and stir in the oil or butter and serve.

baking afternoon

This is where most children start to learn the pleasure of cooking—making gingerbread people, cupcakes, or a birthday cake for someone special. No wonder this is what we remember with fondness; the afternoons spent squeezing doughs, cutting out shapes, pressing on colorful decorations, watching through the glass door of the oven as the aromas fill up the kitchen, then eating the results. There are recipes for the youngest children to play with, and more challenging ones for those keen to experiment with yeast doughs.

gingerbread people

2⅓ cups self-rising flour

a pinch of salt

1 tablespoon ground ginger

1 cup sugar

1 stick unsalted butter

¼ cup light corn syrup

1 extra-large egg

To decorate

raisins

edible silver balls

mini-M&Ms®

2 baking sheets

shaped cookie cutters

**MAKES 14 FIGURES,
5 INCHES LONG**

Don't just make little people—look for cutters in the shape of a princess, a pony, teddy bear, or Santa. Decorate them with chocolate chips, M&Ms®, or raisins.

1 ASK AN ADULT TO HELP YOU preheat the oven to 325°F. Grease several baking sheets with soft butter, using a piece of paper towel.

2 Set a sieve over a large bowl. Tip the flour, salt, and ground ginger into the sieve and sift into the bowl. Add the sugar and mix in with a wooden spoon. Make a hollow in the center of the flour.

3 Put the butter and syrup into a small saucepan. ASK AN ADULT TO HELP YOU melt the butter and corn syrup gently over very low heat—warm the pan just enough to melt the ingredients, don't let the mixture become hot.

4 Carefully pour the melted mixture into the hollow in the flour.

5 Crack the egg into a small bowl and break up with a fork.

6 Pour the egg into the hollow on top of the melted mixture. Mix all the ingredients with a wooden spoon. As soon as the dough starts to come together, put your hands into the bowl and start to push the barely warm dough together. If the dough is too hot to handle, wait for it to cool.

7 As soon as the dough has come together into a ball, and is no longer crumbly, tip it out of the bowl and onto a work surface lightly dusted with flour.

8 With a rolling pin, gently roll out the dough to a large rectangle about ¼-inch thick.

9 Cut out figures with your cutters, then carefully transfer them to the prepared baking sheets with a large spatula. Don't worry if their limbs or heads fall off—just press them back together again. Space the figures well apart, because they will spread in the oven. Gather all the trimmings into a ball, then roll out and cut more figures as before.

10 Decorate the figures with raisins, silver balls or Mini-Smarties®. ASK AN ADULT TO HELP YOU bake the figures—they will take about 15 minutes until golden brown. Watch them carefully, because they can quickly burn.

11 ASK AN ADULT TO HELP YOU remove the trays carefully from the oven and leave them on a heatproof work surface to cool for 5 minutes. This lets the soft cookie mixture become hard. When the figures are firm, gently lift them onto a wire rack, using a large spatula. Let them cool completely.

12 Store in an airtight container and eat within 1 week.

Everybody loves chocolate muffins! These are quick-mix and made with cocoa powder plus chocolate chips for maximum chocolate flavor.

double chocolate muffins

1¾ cups all-purpose flour

½ cup unsweetened cocoa powder

2 teaspoons baking powder

½ cup sugar

½ cup semi-sweet chocolate chips

2 extra-large eggs

1 cup milk

½ cup safflower oil

1 teaspoon pure vanilla extract

2 tablespoons chocolate chips, for sprinkling

a 12-cup deep muffin pan

muffin papers

a wire rack

MAKES 12

1 ASK AN ADULT TO HELP YOU preheat the oven to 400°F.

2 Put a muffin paper in each cup of a 12-cup deep muffin pan.

3 Set a large sieve over a large bowl. Tip the flour, cocoa, baking powder, and sugar into the sieve and sift into the bowl. Add the chocolate chips.

4 Break the eggs into a large bowl. Add the milk, oil, and vanilla, then mix well with a fork. Add the flour mixture and gently stir with a wooden spoon.

5 Spoon the mixture into the muffin papers—each one will be about half full. Carefully dot with chocolate chips.

6 ASK AN ADULT TO HELP YOU put the muffin pan into the hot oven. Cook them for about 20 minutes until well-risen and just firm. The chocolate chips become very hot, so take care not to touch them.

7 ASK AN ADULT TO HELP YOU to remove the pan carefully from the oven. Take the muffins out of the hot pan and put them onto a wire rack to cool. This should take about 30 minutes.

8 These muffins are best eaten the same day. However, when cool, the muffins can be into freezer bags or a plastic container and frozen for up to 1 month.

This wonderfully fudgy cake is perfect for a birthday or any other party. Like all chocolate cakes, this one is best if you make it the day before you plan to eat it.

best-ever chocolate cake

½ **cup sugar**

1 stick unsalted butter, at room temperature, plus extra for greasing the cake pans

½ **teaspoon vanilla extract**

2 extra large eggs, at room temperature

1 cup sour cream, at room temperature

1¾ cups all-purpose flour

½ **cup unsweetened cocoa powder**

1 teaspoon baking powder

1 teaspoon baking soda

a pinch of salt

chocolate frosting

6 oz. best-quality milk chocolate

3½ oz. semi-sweet chocolate

1 cup sour cream

2 cake pans,
8 inches diameter

nonstick parchment paper or
waxed paper

wire rack

SERVES 8 TO 10

1 ASK AN ADULT TO HELP YOU preheat the oven to 350°F.

2 Grease the insides of the cake pans with a small amount of very soft butter on a piece of paper towel. Cut out 2 circles from a sheet of nonstick baking paper or waxed paper—put the cake pan on the paper and draw around it. Using shears, cut inside the line so you have 2 circles the same size as the pans. Fit them into the bottom of each pan.

3 Put the sugar, soft butter, and vanilla in a large bowl. Break the eggs into the bowl, then add the sour cream.

4 Set a large sieve over the bowl and tip the flour, cocoa powder, baking powder, baking soda, and salt into the sieve. Carefully sift these ingredients into the bowl.

5 Using a wooden spoon or electric hand mixer (use slow speed), beat the mixture for about 1 minute until thoroughly smooth.

6 Spoon the mixture into the 2 pans so they are evenly filled, then spread the mixture so it is smooth.

7 ASK AN ADULT TO HELP YOU put the cakes in the oven. Bake them for 20 minutes, then carefully remove from the oven. Turn the cakes upside down onto the wire rack. The cakes will drop out, and you can peel off the lining paper and let them cool.

8 To make the frosting, break up the chocolate bars and put into a heatproof bowl. ASK AN ADULT TO HELP YOU heat some water in a medium saucepan, then remove the pan from the heat as the water boils. Set the bowl over the pan of hot water and let the chocolate melt, stirring every minute.

9 When the chocolate has melted, carefully remove the bowl from the pan. Let the chocolate cool for 5 minutes, then gently stir in the sour cream to make a smooth, thick frosting.

10 Set one of the cakes on a serving plate. Spread about one-third of the frosting over the cake, then set the second cake gently on top of the first. Spread the rest of the frosting on the top and sides of the cake to cover it completely. Leave in a cool spot until firm before you cut it—the cake is best if stored in an airtight container and cut the next day.

Unwaxed lemons are best
if you can find them,
because you need both
the skin and juice for this
simple but tangy loaf cake.

lemon drizzle loaf cake

1½ sticks unsalted butter, very soft,
plus extra for the pan

1¼ cups sugar

2 unwaxed lemons

3 extra large eggs, at room temperature

1¾ cups self–rising flour

½ teaspoon baking powder

½ cup milk, at room temperature

½ cup sugar, to make the drizzle topping

a large loaf pan, about 16 x 5 x 4 inches

waxed paper or nonstick parchment paper

a wire rack

MAKES 1 LARGE CAKE

1 ASK AN ADULT TO HELP YOU preheat the oven to 350°F.

2 Lightly rub the inside of the loaf pan with a little soft butter and a paper towel. Cut a long strip of waxed paper or nonstick parchment paper the width of the pan. Press the paper into the pan so it covers the base and the 2 short sides. Cut some more paper and do the same for the long sides.

3 Put the soft butter and sugar in a large bowl.

4 Rinse the lemons, then grate the yellow zest straight into the bowl using a lemon zester or fine grater.

5 Crack the eggs into the bowl.

6 Set a sieve over the bowl, put the flour and baking powder in it, then sift into the bowl. Add the milk, then beat with a wooden spoon or electric hand mixer (on low speed) for 1 minute until smooth and well mixed, with no streaks of flour.

7 Spoon the mixture into the prepared pan and spread the surface to make it smooth.

8 ASK AN ADULT TO HELP YOU put the pan in the heated oven. Bake the loaf for 50 to 55 minutes. To test if the loaf is cooked, carefully remove it from the oven, then push a toothpick into the center of the loaf. If the toothpick comes out clean, the loaf is ready. If it is sticky with mixture, then cook the loaf for another 5 minutes.

9 While the loaf is cooking, make the topping. Cut the lemons in half and squeeze out the juice with a lemon squeezer. Pour the juice into a small bowl. Add the sugar and stir for 1 minute to make a syrupy glaze.

10 When the loaf is cooked, carefully remove it from the oven and stand the pan on a wire cooling rack. Prick the top of the loaf all over with a toothpick to make lots of small holes in the cake. Spoon the lemon syrup all over the cake so it trickles into the holes in the cake. Leave until completely cold before lifting the cake out of the pan. Peel off the lining paper and cut the loaf into thick slices.

11 Store in an airtight container and eat within 4 days.

Perfect for picnics and lunchboxes, and you can add your favorite nuts or dried fruit.

toffee loaf cake

2 cups all-purpose flour

1 teaspoon baking soda

1 cup firmly packed brown sugar

½ cup plain yogurt

½ cup milk

1 extra large egg

1½ tablespoons unsalted butter, plus extra for greasing

½ cup chopped pecans, mixed nuts, or raisins

*a loaf pan
(8½ x 4½ x 2½ inches)*

nonstick parchment paper or waxed paper

a wire rack

MAKES 1 MEDIUM CAKE

1 ASK AN ADULT TO HELP YOU preheat the oven to 350°F.

2 Lightly grease the pan with soft butter and a paper towel, then cut a strip of waxed paper the width of the pan and about 14–15 inches long. Fit the paper into the base of the pan so it covers the 2 short sides.

3 Put the flour, baking soda, and sugar in a bowl.

4 Spoon the yogurt into a measuring cup, then top up with the milk (to make 1 cup). Break the egg into the cup and stir well with a fork.

5 To melt the butter, ASK AN ADULT TO HELP. Either put it in a small saucepan over the lowest possible heat, or put it in a microwave-proof dish and microwave on MEDIUM for about 20 seconds, then pour into the cup.

6 Pour the liquids in the cup into the bowl. Mix well with a wooden spoon for 1 minute, then mix in the nuts or raisins.

7 Spoon the mixture into the pan. ASK AN ADULT TO HELP YOU put the pan into the hot oven. Bake for 45 to 50 minutes until golden brown. To test if the cake is cooked in the middle, push a toothpick into the center of the cake, then gently pull it out. If the toothpick is clean, then the cake is cooked; if it is coated in cake mix, then cook for about 5 minutes more.

8 ASK AN ADULT TO HELP YOU remove the pan from the oven and put it on a wire rack to cool. Leave for 10 minutes, then lift the loaf out of the pan using the lining paper. Leave until cold on the wire rack. Serve thickly sliced.

9 Store in an airtight container. Eat within 4 days or freeze for up to 1 month.

These smell and taste wonderful. The recipe is traditional and simple, but the lemon zest makes it extra special. Eat biscuits warm with butter.

lemon and thyme biscuits

1 ASK AN ADULT TO HELP YOU preheat the oven to 425°F. Rub the baking sheet with a little soft butter on a paper towel.

2 Put the flour and sugar in a medium bowl.

3 Rinse the lemon under cold running water, then dry with paper towels. Grate off the yellow zest with a lemon zester or the fine side of a kitchen grater. Put the lemon zest and thyme leaves into the bowl and mix all the ingredients well with your hand.

4 Using an ordinary table knife, cut the butter into tiny pieces and add to the bowl.

5 Toss the pieces of butter in the flour so they are well coated, then rub the butter into the flour—to do this, pick up a handful of the mixture with your fingers, then rub the mixture between the very ends of your fingers so the bits of butter become smaller and smaller as they mix with the flour. Keep rubbing in until the whole mixture looks like crumbs. Make a hollow in the center of the crumby mixture.

6 Crack the egg into a measuring cup. Mix with a fork, just enough to break up the yolk and the white. Add enough milk to make up to ⅔ cup.

7 Pour three-quarters of the milk mixture into the hollow. Using the table knife, stir the liquid and flour mixture together to make a soft, coarse-looking dough. If the dough is dry and crumbly, and won't stick together, stir in more of the milk mixture, 1 tablespoon at a time.

8 Tip the dough out of the bowl and onto a work surface lightly covered with flour.

1⅔ cups self-rising flour

3 tablespoons sugar

1 unwaxed lemon

a big pinch of fresh thyme leaves

3 tablespoons unsalted butter, plus extra for the baking sheet

1 extra-large egg

about ⅓ cup milk

a baking sheet

a round cookie cutter, about 2 inches, or a drinking glass the same diameter

a wire rack

MAKES 8

9 Work and knead the ball of dough with your hands for a few seconds so it looks smoother. Dip your hands in a little more flour, then pat out the ball of dough until it is about ½ inch thick. Dip the cookie cutter in flour, then cut out rounds. Gather up all the scraps of dough into a ball, then pat out again and cut more rounds.

10 Put all the rounds on the greased baking sheet, arranging them slightly apart.

11 ASK AN ADULT TO HELP YOU put the tray into the hot oven, then bake for 10 to 12 minutes until golden brown.

12 AGAIN WITH ADULT HELP, carefully remove the tray from the oven and set it on a heatproof surface. Transfer the biscuits to a wire rack with a metal spatula. Let cool until warm, then serve.

13 Best eaten the same day. They can also be toasted.

Another way

• You can also make biscuits in a food processor. Put the flour, sugar, lemon zest, and thyme in the food processor. ASK AN ADULT TO HELP YOU blend for a few seconds just to mix the ingredients. Add the bits of butter to the bowl and blend again until the mixture looks like crumbs. Pour in three-quarters of the milk and egg mixture and process until the dough comes together in a ball, adding more of the milk mixture as needed. ASK AN ADULT to remove the blade carefully from the processor before you remove the dough. Pat out the dough and cut rounds as before.

Just a little spicy, these biscuits are good to eat warm with soup or salad. An easy way to grate cheese is to use a rotary grater, if you use a kitchen grater, take care you don't grate your fingers too—it's sharp.

cheese and chile biscuits

1⅔ cups self-rising flour

a big pinch of salt

a big pinch of freshly ground black pepper

a big pinch of crushed hot red pepper flakes

3 tablespoons unsalted butter, plus extra for greasing the tray

¼ cup freshly grated aged sharp Cheddar cheese or jack cheese

1 extra large egg

about ⅓ cup milk

2 tablespoons grated cheese, for topping

a baking sheet

MAKES 8

1 ASK AN ADULT TO HELP YOU preheat the oven to 425°F. Put a little bit of butter on a paper towel and rub it all over the baking sheet. This is called "greasing," and it keeps the biscuits from sticking to the sheet.

2 Put the flour, salt, pepper, and pepper flakes in a large bowl and mix well. Using a round-bladed table knife, cut the butter into small pieces, then mix into the flour. Using the tips of your fingers, rub the butter into the flour so the mixture looks like crumbs.

3 Stir in the grated cheese, then make a hollow in the mixture.

4 Crack the egg into a measuring cup, then add enough milk to make up to ⅔ cup. Mix the egg into the milk with a fork, then pour three-quarters of this mixture into the hollow you've made in the bowl of flour.

5 Using a round-bladed table knife, stir the ingredients to make a soft but not too sticky dough. If the dough is stiff, dry, and very crumbly, stir in more of the milk 1 tablespoon at a time.

6 Lightly sprinkle a work surface with flour, then tip out the dough onto the surface. Flour your hands and work the dough into a rough-looking ball. Flatten the ball to make a round about 7 inches across. With a round-bladed table knife, cut the dough into 8 wedges, like a cake. Brush the tops with a little of the leftover milk mixture or use a little extra plain milk. Sprinkle the cheese on the top.

7 Using a metal spatula, lift up the biscuits and put them on the prepared baking tray, spacing them slightly apart. They will expand in the oven and we don't want them to touch each other.

8 ASK AN ADULT TO HELP YOU put the tray into the preheated oven. Bake the biscuits for about 10 minutes until golden brown. WITH ADULT HELP, carefully remove the tray from the oven and transfer the biscuits to a wire rack and leave for a few minutes until just cool enough to eat. Eat with butter.

9 If there are any left over, you can toast them the next day.

It's not difficult to make bread. Not much can go wrong; you can kill the yeast (it's a living fungus believe it or not) with too much heat—if the mixing liquid is too hot for your little finger it's too hot for the yeast—but it can usually stand any amount of handling. This recipe gives you the method for a simple loaf, but you can also make animal shapes, pizzas, or a braid from the same dough. If you feel inspired, you can add fruit and nuts or cheese to the dough.

making bread

2⅓ cups unbleached all-purpose flour

1 teaspoon salt

half a 0.6 oz cake compressed fresh yeast
OR half a ¼ oz. sachet active dry yeast

⅞ cup warm water

butter, for greasing the pan

a loaf pan (8½ x 4½ x 2½ inches), lightly greased

MAKES 1 MEDIUM LOAF

1 Put the flour in a large mixing bowl. Add the salt (and the dry yeast if you are using this), and mix everything with your hand. Make a hollow in the middle of the flour.

2 If you are using fresh yeast, put it in a small bowl and break it into small crumbs with your fingers. Add half the water and stir well with a teaspoon.

3 Pour the yeast liquid into the hollow, then the rest of the water. If you are using the dry yeast pour all the water straight into the well in the flour mixture.

4 Using your hand, slowly stir the flour into the liquid in the hollow—the mixture will turn from a thick batter to a soft dough as more flour is drawn in. Work the mixture with your hand until all the flour has been mixed in—flours vary from brand to brand, so if there are dry crumbs in the bowl and the dough feels very dry and hard to mix, add a little more water to the bowl, 1 tablespoon at a time. If the dough is very sticky and sticks to your fingers or the sides of the bowl, add more flour 1 tablespoon at a time.

5 Sprinkle a little flour over the work surface and tip the dough out of the bowl onto it. Using both hands, knead the dough by stretching it out away from you, then gathering it back into a ball again. Turn the ball around and stretch the dough out again then gather it back into a ball. Keep doing this for about 10 minutes—it's hard work but you can take a short rest every now and then. You can also knead the dough in a large food mixer with the dough hook attachment—it will take 4 minutes on very low speed, ASK AN ADULT TO HELP YOU do this.

6 Put the kneaded dough back in the mixing bowl—it now has to be left to rise. Yeast dough likes to be kept warm and moist, so cover the bowl with a snap-on lid, or put the bowl into a large, clean plastic bag (supermarket bags work well), then tie it closed.

continued

making bread continued

7 If you leave the bowl near a warm stove or above a radiator, it will take about 1 hour to double in size. At normal room temperature it will take 1½ to 2 hours, depending on the time of year. If it's in a cool unheated room, it will 2 to 6 hours, or you can leave it overnight in the refrigerator.

8 While the dough is rising, put some butter on a paper towel and rub it lightly over the inside of the loaf pan. This is called "greasing."

9 When the dough has doubled in size, uncover the bowl, and gently punch down the dough with your fist. Sprinkle your work surface lightly with flour, then tip out the dough onto it. Shape the dough into a brick to fit your pan. Lift the dough into the pan and gently press it in.

10 Put the pan in a plastic bag again, and let the dough rise in a warm place until doubled in size—about 1 hour.

11 While the dough is rising, ASK AN ADULT TO HELP YOU preheat the oven to 425°F.

12 Uncover the risen dough and ASK AN ADULT TO HELP YOU put the pan in the oven. Bake it for 30 minutes until it is golden brown. AGAIN WITH ADULT HELP, carefully remove from the oven and tip the bread out of the pan onto a wire rack to cool.

13 To make sure the bread is cooked right through, carefully tap the underside of the loaf with the back of your hand—it should sound hollow like a drum, if you hear a dull "thump," then put the loaf, without the pan, back in the oven for another 5 minutes, then test again.

14 Let the bread cool on the wire rack before cutting.

15 Eat within 5 days or freeze for up to 1 month.

other breads

The same dough can be made into rolls—when it comes to the shaping part, divide the dough into 8 even pieces. Roll into balls, or sausage shapes, or make into animal shapes with raisin eyes (crocodiles, mice, cats, pigs, snakes, or hedgehogs—you make the spikes by cutting snips into the dough with kitchen shears). Let rise, spaced well apart on 2 greased baking sheets, then bake in the preheated oven for 15 to 20 minutes, depending on the thickness of the rolls.

To make pizza bases—add 1 teaspoon dried oregano to the flour at the same time as the salt, then add 1 tablespoon good olive oil to the water when mixing the dough. When it comes to shaping the dough, divide it into 4 even pieces, then shape each piece into a ball. Flatten each ball to a round about 7 inches across. Put the pizza bases on 2 baking sheets, spaced well apart. Let rise for about 20 minutes while you prepare the topping (see the recipe on page 40).

To make a braided loaf—mix the dough with tepid milk instead of water. When it comes to shaping the dough, divide the dough into 3 equal pieces. Using your hands, roll the dough into 3 sausage shapes about 16 inches long. Pinch the 3 strands together at one end, then braid the dough, pinch the other ends together, and tuck underneath. Carefully lift onto a greased baking sheet, then let rise and bake as in the main recipe.

To make shiny bread—just before baking the bread, dip a pastry brush into a little beaten egg or milk and carefully brush over the top of the dough, but don't let it drip onto the pan or the sheet or the dough will be "glued" on, and be difficult to remove after baking. If the dough is glazed in this way, you can sprinkle it with sesame seeds, poppy seeds, sunflower seeds, or grated cheese and they will stick to the dough.

To make cheese bread—add 1 cup grated Cheddar cheese to the flour at the same time as the salt.

My son Dan started making this wonderful golden bread when he was six. It's a great recipe for new bakers—the dough can be kneaded in an electric mixer using a dough hook, and it only needs one rising in the pan—so no shaping needed! It's done in stages, so read the whole recipe before you start. Eat the bread thickly sliced, with or without butter, or toasted for breakfast or at tea time. (It's called Cornish bread because saffron used to be grown in Cornwall, England.)

cornish bread

½ teaspoon saffron strands

1¼ cups milk

4 cups unbleached white bread flour

1 teaspoon salt

1 stick plus 3 tablespoons unsalted butter, plus extra for greasing the pan

¼ cup firmly packed brown sugar

0.6 oz cake compressed fresh yeast or 1 envelope (2½ teaspoons) rapid-rise active dry yeast

⅔ cup mixed dried fruit (golden raisins, raisins, and currants)

a loaf pan (8½ x 4½ x 2½ inches), greased with butter and gently warmed

MAKES 1 MEDIUM LOAF

1 Pick up the strands of saffron and rub them between your fingers into a heatproof pitcher. ASK AN ADULT TO HELP YOU heat up the milk in a small saucepan or in the microwave for 2 minutes on HIGH until it is very hot but not boiling. Carefully pour the milk onto the saffron, then cover the pitcher with a saucer or small plate and set aside to infuse (this means to let the milk absorb the flavor and color of the saffron) for 2 to 4 hours. You don't have to stay while this happens.

2 Put the flour and salt in a bowl or the bowl of an electric mixer. If you are using active dry yeast, add it now. Mix the flour and salt with your hand. Cut the butter into small pieces with a round-bladed table knife and put them in the bowl. Toss the pieces of butter in the flour so they are coated in flour. Then pick up a handful of the mix and rub it between your fingers so it falls back into the bowl. This is quite a sticky business, but after about 5 minutes, the lumps of butter will have been crushed and mixed with the flour. Keep rubbing the butter into the flour until the mixture looks like bread crumbs. Mix in the sugar.

3 ASK AN ADULT to warm up the milk gently—it should just feel comfortable to touch.

4 If you are using fresh yeast, crumble it between your fingers into the milk and stir well.

5 With your hands, make a hollow in the middle of the flour mixture, then pour in the warm saffron milk. Mix with your hands until you have a heavy, sticky dough.

6 Sprinkle your work surface with flour, then lift the dough out of the bowl onto the work surface. Knead the dough, stretching it out, then gathering it back into a ball. Do this for 5 minutes, though you can take a rest now and again. At the end, the dough will feel much more elastic and springy. Alternatively, if you have a large electric mixer, knead the dough using the dough hook attachment for 4 to 5 minutes on the lowest speed—ASK AN ADULT FOR HELP in setting this up.

7 When you have finished kneading, sprinkle the fruit onto the dough. Mix it in with your hands by squeezing the dough through your fingers.

8 Lift the dough into the warm pan, pressing it down well to squeeze out the air bubbles.

9 Put the pan into a large plastic bag and gently inflate the bag to make a tent, so the plastic doesn't touch the dough. Tie the ends closed, then leave in a warm place until the dough has risen to the top of the pan—about 1 hour. Meanwhile ASK AN ADULT TO HELP YOU preheat the oven to 350°F.

10 Remove the loaf from the plastic tent and ASK AN ADULT TO HELP YOU put the loaf in the oven. Bake it for about 1 hour until a good golden brown. Again, WITH ADULT HELP, remove the loaf from the oven and tip it upside down onto the wire rack. Tap the underside of the loaf with the back of your knuckles—if there is a hollow drum-like sound the loaf is cooked. If there is a heavy, dull thump, put the loaf back in the oven for another 5 minutes.

11 Let cool completely before slicing. Best eaten within 4 days or freeze for up to 1 month.

The best recipe for your first-ever loaf—we call it "Honey I'm whole wheat!" It was invented accidentally by Doris Grant about 60 years ago and proves that sometimes accidents taste good. Unlike most bread doughs, this one is not kneaded or shaped and has only one rising—in the pan. The Grant Loaf makes great sandwiches and toast, and is lovely with cheese or soup. Tip: with bread making, it's a good idea to use cold water for cleaning up (otherwise you'll get wallpaper glue).

the grant loaf

5 cups stoneground
whole wheat bread flour

1 teaspoon salt

0.6 oz cake compressed fresh yeast
or 1 envelope (2½ teaspoons) active dry
yeast

1 tablespoon honey

2½ cups tepid water

butter, for greasing

*a large loaf pan, about 16 x 5 x 4 inches,
greased with butter*

MAKES 1 LARGE LOAF

1 Put the flour and salt in a large bowl (stand the bowl on a damp dish towel to keep it from wobbling) and mix well with your hand. If using dry yeast, mix it in now.

2 Put the fresh yeast in a small bowl and crumble it with your fingers. Put the honey in the bowl with about ½ cup of the warm water. Mix with a teaspoon until smooth.

3 Use your hand to make a hollow in the center of the flour. Pour the yeast liquid into the hollow, then the rest of the water. Leave for 5 minutes—the yeast liquid will become very bubbly. If using dry yeast, add the honey and water and continue with the recipe.

4 Mix the flour into the liquid with your hand, then mix well for 1 minute, moving the dough from the sides of the bowl into the center. Mix 1 more minute until the dough feels very slippery and elastic and comes cleanly away from the sides of the bowl.

5 Lift the dough into the pan and smooth the surface with a plastic spatula. Cover loosely with a clean, damp dish towel. Leave in a warm spot for 30 to 40 minutes or until the dough rises to within ½ inch of the top of the pan. While the dough is rising, ASK AN ADULT TO HELP YOU heat the oven to 400°F.

6 ASK AN ADULT TO HELP YOU put the loaf pan into the oven. Bake it for about 35 to 40 minutes.

7 To test if the loaf is cooked, ASK AN ADULT TO HELP YOU remove the pan from the oven. Using oven mitts or a thick pot holder to protect your hands, remove the loaf from the pan and tap it underneath. If it sounds hollow, like a drum, then the loaf is cooked. If it sounds like a dead thump, then return it to the oven for another 5 minutes.

8 Transfer the loaf to a wire rack until cold.

9 Best eaten within 4 days or freeze for up to 1 month.

Another idea
• Add 1 or 2 tablespoons sunflower seeds or pumpkin seeds to the dough when you add the salt.

We always seem to have extra bodies to feed at weekends, so everyone helps with Saturday dinner and Sunday lunch, from planning menus to shopping, setting the table, cooking, then finally serving to a round of applause (don't mention the washing up). Each child has a special menu—for Stevie it's always Bang Bang Chicken, made exactly as they do in her favorite Chinese restaurant. Dan likes to enjoy a roast lunch on Sunday, so he makes Italian Chicken Legs with roast vegetables, followed by meringues. Emily is still hooked on pancakes with maple syrup. It's a really fun way to spend time together as a family.

real meals

This is a favorite cold salad from our local Chinese restaurant—ready-cooked smoked or "plain-roast" chicken is arranged on sticks of cucumber then topped with a creamy peanut butter dressing.

bang bang chicken

14 oz. ready-cooked boneless chicken, such as smoked chicken, cold roast chicken, or cold turkey

1 medium cucumber

1 large carrot

salad leaves such as crisp lettuce or Chinese leaves, about 1 cup

Bang bang dressing

5 tablespoons crunchy peanut butter

1 scallion

1 teaspoon sesame oil

1 teaspoon soy sauce

1 teaspoon sugar

1 teaspoon Chinese white rice vinegar or cider vinegar

1 teaspoon rice wine or water

3 tablespoons hot water

SERVES 4

1 Remove any skin from the chicken and discard. Pull or cut the chicken into shreds the size of your little finger, then put onto a plate.

2 Rinse the cucumber. Cut off the ends and discard. Cut the cucumber in half lengthwise, then in half crosswise. Cut each piece into lengthwise slices the width of your little finger. Put on another plate.

3 Peel off the carrot skin with a vegetable peeler, then cut off the ends and discard.

4 Make carrot ribbons by "peeling" the carrot with the peeler to make ultra-thin long strips of carrot.

5 Rinse the salad leaves and dry thoroughly in a salad spinner or pat dry with paper towels. Tear any large leaves into bite-size pieces. Arrange the leaves on a serving dish. Scatter the cucumber sticks and carrot ribbons over the leaves. Lastly, arrange the chicken on the top.

6 To make the dressing, put the peanut butter in a small bowl. Rinse the scallion. With a small knife, cut off the hairy root end and the very dark leaves at the top. Cut the scallion into very thin slices and add to the peanut butter. Add the sesame oil, soy sauce, sugar, vinegar, rice wine or water, and hot water to the bowl. Stir gently until well mixed. Taste the dressing—it should be a harmonious balance of salty, sweet, and sour flavors, so add more vinegar, sugar, or soy as you think is needed. The dressing should be just thin enough to spoon over the chicken, so if it is too thick stir in another tablespoon or so of hot water.

7 When the sauce seems perfect, spoon it over the chicken and serve.

It's hard to resist the smell of roasting chicken and, because this dish uses chicken pieces, there's no difficult carving, and the gravy appears during cooking. Choose organic chicken legs if you're hungry, otherwise large thighs, because these have the most flavor and it's fun to chew the meat off the bones. Serve with Roasties (page 94), or pasta and a green vegetable, or Flag Salad (page 39).

italian roast chicken

4 chicken legs or thighs

4 unpeeled garlic cloves

1 large lemon

2 tablespoons olive oil

sea salt and freshly ground black pepper

4 large sprigs fresh thyme or rosemary

1 or 2 ovenproof baking dishes, big enough to hold the chicken in one layer

SERVES 4

1 ASK AN ADULT TO HELP YOU preheat the oven to 425°F.

2 While the oven heats, get the chicken ready for roasting; you will need ovenproof baking dishes that can also be the serving dishes.

3 Put the chicken pieces straight from the bag they came in into the dishes, skin side facing up, and check that the pieces don't overlap each other. When you've done this, wash your hands thoroughly with soap and hot water. Make sure anything touched by the raw chicken is also thoroughly washed; this is important to avoid the spread of bacteria which could make you ill.

4 Put the garlic cloves in the dishes between the chicken pieces. Cut the lemon in half and squeeze out the juice with a lemon squeezer. Pour the juice over the chicken, then pour the oil over the top so the skin is evenly coated in liquid. Sprinkle with 4 pinches of salt and then about 3 turns of the pepper grinder. Finally, set a sprig of thyme or rosemary on the top of each piece of chicken.

5 ASK AN ADULT to put the baking dishes into the heated oven. Set the timer for 40 minutes for large legs, and 35 minutes for thighs. As the chicken cooks, the legs become a crispy golden brown, surrounded by a light brown cooking-juice gravy.

6 ASK AN ADULT to remove the dishes from the hot oven and put onto the table.

thai meatballs with chicken

Mildly spicy and full of flavor, these chicken balls are made with your hands, then simply baked in the oven—no frying needed. Serve with Thai fragrant rice and extra sweet chile sauce (it's mild, not hot—a bit like Thai tomato ketchup) for dipping.

2 oz. fresh bread (about 2 medium slices)

1 lb. ground chicken or turkey

1 large egg

2 scallions

½ teaspoon ground coriander

a small bunch of fresh cilantro

1 teaspoon Asian fish sauce or soy sauce

2 teaspoons sweet chile sauce, plus extra for serving

vegetable oil, for greasing the dish

a large baking dish

MAKES 12: SERVES 4

1 ASK AN ADULT TO HELP YOU preheat the oven to 400°F.

2 Tear up the bread and put it into a blender or processor. ASK AN ADULT TO HELP YOU process the bread until it turns into crumbs. Tip the crumbs into a bowl. Add the ground chicken or turkey. Crack the egg into the bowl. Wash your hands well after touching raw meat or eggs.

3 Rinse the scallions. Using a small knife, cut off each hairy root end and the very dark leaves at the top. Cut the onions into very thin slices. Add to the bowl, then add the ground coriander. Using kitchen shears, snip the fresh cilantro straight into the bowl. Add the fish sauce or soy sauce and the sweet chile sauce to the bowl. Mix well with your hands then roll the mixture into small balls—use about 1 tablespoon of mixture for each.

4 Rub the base of the baking dish with oil, then arrange the balls in the dish. ASK AN ADULT TO HELP YOU put it into the preheated oven to bake for 25 minutes until golden brown and cooked all the way through.

5 While the meatballs are cooking, wash your hands well, then make the rice (right).

6 Serve the meatballs straight from the baking dish with the rice and extra sweet chile sauce in a small dish for dipping.

thai fragrant rice

1¼ cups Thai fragrant rice

a pinch of salt

ENOUGH FOR 4

1 ASK AN ADULT TO HELP with this recipe, because it involves boiling water.

2 Fill a large saucepan half full with water and put it on the stove. Cover with a lid, then turn on the heat and leave until the water boils (about 5 to 10 minutes).

3 Carefully pour the rice into the water, add the salt, and stir gently. When the water starts to boil again, turn the heat down so the water doesn't bubble over the sides of the pan. Leave to boil gently (this is called simmering) for 10 minutes. Alternatively, follow the directions on the package.

4 Make sure the sink is empty, then set a colander in the middle. ASK AN ADULT to strain the rice through the colander. Shake the colander well to drain off all the water, then tip the rice into a serving bowl and serve straight away with the chicken.

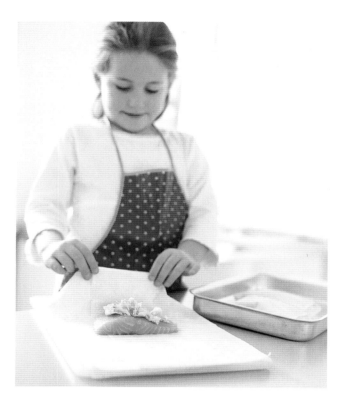

salmon phyllo packages

4 pieces skinless salmon fillet, about 4 oz. each

4 tablespoons unsalted butter, at room temperature

2 small or 1 large piece of ginger preserved in syrup

sea salt and freshly ground black pepper

8 oz. phyllo pastry dough, thawed if necessary

1 lemon, to serve

vegetable oil, for greasing

a large ovenproof baking dish

MAKES 4

Phyllo pastry is easy to use. You don't have to mix it or roll it out—just don't uncover it until the last moment or it will get very dry. In this recipe, boneless, skinless pieces of salmon are topped with a gingery butter (made with ginger preserved in syrup, from the Asian section of the supermarket) then wrapped up in phyllo, and baked.

1 ASK AN ADULT TO HELP YOU preheat the oven to 375°F.

2 Lightly grease the baking dish or roasting pan with a little vegetable oil on a piece of paper towel.

3 Rinse the 4 pieces of salmon under cold running water, then pat dry with paper towels.

4 Put the butter in a small bowl and stir with a teaspoon until soft. Lift the ginger out of the syrup and onto a small plate. Using a small knife, cut the ginger into thin slices. then cut the slices into strips. Add the ginger to the butter, then add the salt and pepper and mix well. Divide the mixture into 4 equal pieces.

5 Unwrap the phyllo pastry dough and separate and count the sheets. You will need an equal number for each package. Brands of phyllo vary from store to store, and each brand has different-size sheets, but arrange the sheets to make 4 rectangles, about 12 x 10 inches by overlapping or folding the sheets. If you have to cut sheets in half, use kitchen shears.

6 Put a piece of fish right in the middle of each rectangle. Spread the top of each piece of fish with a piece of the butter. Fold the phyllo over the fish as if you were wrapping up a Christmas gift, then fold the ends underneath. Arrange the packages in the prepared dish, then ASK AN ADULT TO HELP YOU put the dish in the oven.

7 Bake in the preheated oven for 25 minutes until golden brown. ASK AN ADULT TO HELP YOU take the dish out of the oven.

8 Serve the packages hot on 4 plates, together with the lemon cut into 4 wedges.

beef rendang

1 lb. steak for stewing

1 tablespoon tamarind paste

1 cinnamon stick

1 tablespoon brown sugar

2 tablespoons soy sauce

1 cup unsalted beef or vegetable stock

¼ teaspoon ground black pepper

¼ teaspoon freshly grated nutmeg

6 green cardamom pods

2 medium red onions

3 garlic cloves

1 inch piece of fresh ginger

SERVES 4

Not all curry is mouth-stingingly hot. This is a gentle, aromatic, meat curry from Indonesia made all in one pot, with cubes of beef. Tamarind paste is sold in small jars from supermarkets or Asian stores. Serve with Thai fragrant rice (page 89) and green beans.

1 Put the meat in a heavy medium saucepan or casserole dish. Add the tamarind, cinnamon stick, sugar, soy sauce, stock, pepper, and nutmeg.

2 Crush the cardamom pods with a mortar and pestle (or with the end of a rolling pin). Throw away the green husks and keep the tiny black seeds. Crush the seeds and add to the pan.

3 Peel the onions, garlic, and ginger. Cut each onion in 4 and cut the ginger into thick slices. Put the onions, garlic, and ginger in a food processor or blender and ASK AN ADULT TO HELP YOU blend the mixture until it is very finely chopped, almost a coarse purée.

4 Spoon this mixture into a saucepan. Stir gently until well mixed.

5 Set the pan over medium heat and bring the mixture to a boil. ASK AN ADULT TO HELP YOU stir gently and carefully, then cover the pan with a lid and turn down the heat to very low so the mixture bubbles very gently.

6 Let cook for 1½ hours, stirring now and then. You don't have to stay all the time it's cooking. In fact, you could ask an adult to do the stirring. Finally, remove the lid and cook uncovered for 20 to 30 minutes until the sauce is very thick. Remove the cinnamon stick and serve.

It's hard to imagine a roast dinner without crunchy roast potatoes, not to mention roast sweet potatoes, roast parsnips, and more. So here is an easy way to cook all your favorite vegetables in one roasting pan.

roasties

1 lb. baking potatoes

1 lb. parsnips

1 lb. sweet potatoes

1 lb. large carrots

3 tablespoons virgin olive oil

a big pinch of sea salt

several grinds of black pepper

3 sprigs of thyme or rosemary (or both)

a large roasting pan

SERVES 4 TO 6

1 ASK AN ADULT TO HELP YOU preheat the oven to 425°F (the oven may already be on if you are cooking a roast chicken or meat).

2 Peel all the vegetables with a vegetable peeler. Using a medium sharp knife, cut off the ends of the parsnips and carrots, then carefully cut all the vegetables into similar-size chunks. They shouldn't be too neat and even, but aim for chunks about 1½ inches long.

3 Put all the vegetables in a large roasting pan. Pour the oil over the top, sprinkle with the salt and pepper, then add the herbs, pushing them between the vegetables.

4 Using both hands, toss the vegetables in the oil and seasonings so they are very well mixed. Spread out the vegetables so they are in a single layer.

5 ASK AN ADULT TO HELP YOU put the vegetables into the hot oven. Cook for about 1 hour, but every 15 minutes during the cooking time, ASK AN ADULT TO HELP YOU remove the tray carefully from the oven and gently turn over the vegetables so they cook and brown evenly (the cut surface next to the metal tray cooks quickest).

6 At the end of the cooking time, ASK AN ADULT TO HELP YOU remove the tray carefully from the oven. Transfer the roasties to a serving dish, removing any twiggy bits of the herbs. Serve immediately.

corn-on-the-cob

For each ear of corn you will need:

1 tablespoon unsalted butter

a little salt and freshly ground black pepper

an ovenproof dish big enough to fit the corn in a single layer

metal cooking tongs

SERVES 1

Corn is nicest eaten as soon as possible after picking. You don't always have to cook it in boiling water. Grilling is good, but roasting in the oven is just wonderful. How many can you eat?

1 ASK AN ADULT TO HELP YOU preheat the oven to 400°F.

2 If the corn still has its green leafy covering, it must be shucked—pull off the leaves from the pointy top end, then pull off all the silky hairs.

3 To melt the butter, ASK AN ADULT TO HELP. Either put it in a small saucepan over the lowest possible heat, or put it in a microwave-proof dish and microwave on MEDIUM for about 20 seconds.

4 Pour the melted butter into the baking dish and add a big pinch of salt and pepper for each ear of corn. Put the corn into the dish, then rotate them in the butter mix so they are well coated.

5 ASK AN ADULT TO HELP YOU cook the corn in the heated oven—this will take 30 minutes. ASK AN ADULT TO HELP YOU turn the corn over twice carefully during this time—metal cooking tongs are the best thing to use.

6 The corn will be very lightly browned, and too hot to eat immediately, so let them cool for 5 to 10 minutes after they come out of the oven.

Also known as "fruit salad on a stick." You can use your favorite fruits for these brochettes, as long as you can thread them onto bamboo skewers. Choose a good mix of colors and textures like kiwifruit, bananas, peaches, strawberries, or different kinds of melon, depending on what's in season. Use this as a guide.

fresh fruit brochettes

2 kiwis

1 large or 2 small bananas

1 peach or nectarine

16 strawberries

8 bamboo skewers

SERVES 4

1 Peel the kiwis with a vegetable peeler.

2 Put them on a clean board and carefully cut in half with a small sharp knife.

3 Turn the fruit cut side down onto the board then cut each half into 4 wedges.

4 Peel the banana(s) and cut into a total of 8 chunks.

5 Rinse the peach or nectarine under a cold tap. Slice in half from top to bottom, then twist to separate the halves. Ease out the seed, then turn the halves cut side down on the board and slice each half into 4 wedges.

6 Wipe the strawberries with a clean, soft towel. Remove the leaves if you wish.

7 Carefully thread the fruit onto the skewers starting and finishing up with a strawberry so each skewer has 2 strawberries, a wedge each of kiwifruit and peach and a chunk of banana.

8 Eat carefully so the juice doesn't drip down your chin.

When my niece was 10 she had a "cooking" birthday party sleepover. She chose pizza and these pretty tarts, and each guest made her own dinner. The tart base is a rich shortbread, and the topping consists of small fresh strawberries brushed with hot jelly to make a glossy professional glaze. Younger children will need adult help with baking.

little strawberry tarts

Tart base

1²/₃ cups all-purpose flour

¹/₂ cup confectioners' sugar

1¹/₂ sticks unsalted butter, straight from refrigerator

2 extra-large egg yolks

¹/₂ teaspoon pure vanilla extract

Strawberry topping

2 pints small fresh strawberries

about ²/₃ cup raspberry jelly

2 or 3 baking sheets

a pastry brush

MAKES 4 TO 6

1 Put the flour and confectioners' sugar into a large sieve set over a bowl and sift to remove any lumps. Tip the mixture into a food processor. Cut the cold butter into small cubes and add to the flour and confectioners' sugar. ASK AN ADULT TO HELP YOU turn on the processor and blend the mixture until there are no large lumps and it looks like fine bread crumbs. Add the 2 egg yolks and vanilla. Blend the processor again until the dough sticks together in a ball shape. ASK AN ADULT TO HELP YOU remove the dough from the processor (the blade is dangerous), then wrap the dough in plastic wrap or waxed paper and chill in the refrigerator for 30 minutes.

2 The dough can make 4 large or 6 smaller individual tarts, so divide it into 4 or 6 equal pieces as needed. Put a little bit of butter on a paper towel and rub it all over the baking sheets to grease them.

3 Roll each piece of dough into a ball with your hands. Put on the baking sheets, setting them well apart (they will spread in the oven). With your fingers, press and pat out the dough to make circles about ¼ inch thick. You will have either 4 circles, 2¼ inches across, or 6 circles, 4 inches across. Pinch the edges with your fingertips to make a pretty shape, then prick the bases all over with a fork (the tiny air holes will stop the base bubbling up in the oven). Chill in the refrigerator for 10 minutes.

4 Meanwhile, ASK AN ADULT TO HELP YOU preheat the oven to 350°F.

5 ASK AN ADULT TO HELP YOU bake the circles for 20 minutes until they are a light golden color. Carefully remove the sheets from the oven and let the circles cool on the sheets.

6 Check the strawberries and discard any bruised ones. Rinse in a colander and pat dry with paper towels. Remove the green stems and leaves with your fingers or with a small knife.

7 Spoon the jelly into a small saucepan. Add 1 tablespoon of water and ASK AN ADULT TO HELP YOU heat it very gently, stirring with a wooden spoon. The solid jelly will melt and become a thick, smooth, hot syrup. Remove from the heat before it starts to boil.

8 Set each cooked tart crust on a serving plate. Using a pastry brush, brush a little hot jelly over each circle. Arrange the strawberries on the crust with their pointy ends up. Brush the berries with the hot glaze to coat them completely. If the glaze starts to set before you've finished, gently warm it again.

9 Leave until set—about 20 minutes—before serving. Best eaten the same day.

You'll need a rotary beater or electric hand mixer to beat the egg whites to a stiff snow. Serve the crunchy meringues with a mixture of fresh red berries in summer, or frozen ones in winter.

cinnamon meringues with fresh fruit

Meringues

2 egg whites

a pinch of cream of tartar (optional)

½ cup sugar

¼ teaspoon ground cinnamon

nonstick parchment paper

2 baking sheets

Fruit salad

⅓ cup blueberries

⅓ cup raspberries

1 cup small strawberries

1 tablespoon confectioners' sugar

vanilla ice cream, to serve

SERVES 4 TO 6

1 ASK AN ADULT TO HELP YOU preheat the oven to 250°F.

2 Cut out 2 rectangles of nonstick parchment paper to fit the 2 baking sheets, then set one on each sheet.

3 Put the egg whites and cream of tartar in a large, spotlessly clean, and grease-free bowl (grease will make it difficult to beat the whites). Stand the bowl on a damp cloth to keep it from wobbling.

4 Using a rotary or electric hand mixer, start beating the egg whites. Beat steadily until the whites turn into a stiff white foam—lift out the beaters and there will be a little peak of white standing on the end.

5 Mix the sugar with the cinnamon, then beat it into the egg whites, 1 tablespoon at a time, to make a stiff glossy golden meringue.

6 Scoop 1 heaping teaspoon of the mixture out of the bowl, then use a second teaspoon to help you push the meringue onto the prepared sheet to make a craggy mountain-like heap. Scoop out the rest of the mixture in the same way to make about 16 heaps, spaced slightly apart on the sheets.

7 ASK AN ADULT TO HELP YOU put the baking sheets into the hot oven. Bake for 2 hours. Carefully remove the sheets from the oven and let cool. Peel the meringues off the lining paper and pile them up in a serving bowl. The meringues can also be stored in an airtight container for up to 1 week.

8 To make the fruit salad using fresh fruit, rinse the blueberries in a colander under cold running water. Drain thoroughly, then tip into a serving bowl. Add the raspberries, rinse the strawberries, and pull out the green leafy tops. Put two-thirds of the strawberries in the bowl with the other berries. Put the rest of the strawberries in a small bowl, add the sugar, and mash the berries with a fork to make a coarse, juicy purée. Tip this mixture into the bowl of berries and stir gently until just mixed. Cover and leave at room temperature until ready to serve, up to 2 hours.

9 If you are making the salad with frozen fruit, put all the frozen berries and the sugar in a serving bowl. Mix gently, then cover and set aside to defrost slowly, 2 to 4 hours.

10 Serve the meringues and fruit salad with vanilla ice cream.

Lovely at any time of year, this dessert is a combination of juicy fruits and a crunchy topping. Eat warm or cold with ice cream or yogurt.

juicy fruit crisp

2 large Granny Smith, 2 peaches, or 2 medium pears

1⅔ cups fresh or frozen (don't thaw) raspberries, blueberries, or blackberries

2 tablespoons white or brown sugar

Crisp topping

1 cup all-purpose flour

⅓ cup brown sugar

6½ tablespoons unsalted butter, plus extra for greasing the dish

a medium ovenproof baking dish

SERVES 4

1 ASK AN ADULT TO HELP YOU preheat the oven to 375°F.

2 Lightly grease the baking dish by rubbing a little butter over the base and sides.

3 Peel the apples or pears (there is no need to peel peaches) with a vegetable peeler. Cut out the core with an apple corer or by cutting the fruit into quarters, then cutting out the core with a small knife. Cut the peaches in half, then twist to separate the halves— the seed may come out easily, if not cut the peach away from the seed. Discard the skin and cores, then cut the apples, pears, or peaches into chunks the size of half your thumb.

4 Put the fruit in the dish, then add the berries. Sprinkle with the sugar and toss gently until just mixed. Spread the fruit evenly in the dish.

5 To make the topping, put the flour and sugar in a large bowl. Cut the butter into small pieces and add to the bowl. Using your hands, squeeze the mixture together until it becomes all soft and sticky and there are pea-size lumps of dough. Sprinkle this mixture over the fruit—don't press it down.

6 ASK AN ADULT TO HELP YOU put the dish into the oven. Let it bake for 25 minutes until bubbling and golden on top.

7 ASK AN ADULT TO HELP YOU remove the dish carefully. Eat the crisp hot, warm, or cold.

Ready-made phyllo pastry dough works well here, and it doesn't matter what it looks like when it goes into the oven. When it's baked and dusted with confectioners' sugar, your strudel will taste and look sensational. Choose slightly tart, well-flavored apples.

apple strudel

8 oz. phyllo pastry dough

9 amaretti cookies (1½ oz.)

4 medium apples (1¾ lb.)

a generous ⅓ cup sugar

1½ teaspoons ground cinnamon

4 tablespoons unsalted butter, plus extra for greasing

2 tablespoons slivered almonds or raisins, or dried blueberries

confectioners' sugar, for dusting

a large baking sheet

SERVES 6

1 ASK AN ADULT TO HELP YOU preheat the oven to 400°F. Rub the baking sheet with a little soft butter on a paper towel.

2 If the dough is frozen, let it defrost before using. Do not unwrap the dough until you are ready to use it, because it will dry out and become crumbly.

3 Put the amaretti cookies in a plastic bag and tap carefully with a rolling pin until the cookies have turned into crumbs.

4 Peel the apples with a vegetable peeler, then cut out the cores with an apple corer and cut in four, or cut the apples in quarters then cut out the cores with a small sharp knife. Cut each quarter into 4 slices. Put all the apple slices in a large bowl.

5 Mix the sugar and cinnamon in another bowl.

6 To melt the butter, ASK AN ADULT TO HELP. Either put it in a small saucepan over the lowest possible heat, or put it in a microwave-proof dish and microwave on MEDIUM for about 25 seconds.

7 Unwrap the dough and separate the sheets. Overlap the sheets to make a rectangle about 22 x 28 inches. Using a pastry brush, lightly brush about half the melted butter over the dough. Sprinkle the amaretti crumbs on top, then add the apple slices leaving a clear border of about 2 inches all around the edges. Sprinkle with the sugar and cinnamon mixture, then add the almonds or dried fruit.

8 To roll up the strudel, first fold over the pastry borders along the two short sides, then fold over the pastry border along one long side. Roll up the strudel from this side, and don't worry if the pastry splits and the filling falls out, just push it all back together with your hands. You will need an extra pair of hands and a couple of spatulas to help you transfer the roll to the buttered baking sheet. If the roll is too big for the size of your tray, you may have to curve the roll into a horseshoe shape. Again press it all back together. Brush well with the rest of the melted butter.

9 ASK AN ADULT TO HELP YOU put the strudel into the oven. Bake it for 35 minutes, or until golden brown.

10 ASK AN ADULT TO HELP YOU remove the tray carefully from the oven, then dust confectioners' sugar over the top of the strudel. To do this, you can use a sugar shaker filled with confectioners' sugar, or put 2 tablespoons of confectioners' sugar in a small sieve and sift over the strudel.

11 Cut into thick slices and eat warm or at room temperature with cream or yogurt.

A great mix-and-bake recipe with white chocolate lumps for those who don't or can't eat nuts. For a special birthday meal, serve the brownies warm with vanilla ice cream or the warm fudge sauce below (also great with bananas and ice cream).

brownies and ice cream

1¼ sticks unsalted butter

4 extra-large eggs

1½ cups sugar

1 teaspoon pure vanilla extract

¾ cup unsweetened cocoa powder

1¼ cups all-purpose flour

3½ oz. best-quality white chocolate

vanilla ice cream, to serve

a cake pan, 8 inches square

MAKES 16

1 ASK AN ADULT TO HELP YOU preheat the oven to 325°F.

2 While the oven heats up, cut kitchen foil into a 10-inch square, then press the foil into the cake pan to line the base and the sides.

3 To melt the butter, ASK AN ADULT TO HELP. Either put it in a small saucepan over the lowest possible heat, or put it in a microwave-proof dish and microwave on MEDIUM for about 40 seconds.

4 Crack the eggs into a large bowl. Tip the sugar into the bowl, then add the vanilla. Stir well with a wooden spoon for 1 minute until completely mixed.

5 Pour in the melted butter and stir for another 1 minute.

6 Set a large sieve over the bowl and sift the cocoa and flour onto the egg mixture. Stir well for another 1 minute, getting right down to the bottom of the bowl. When there are no streaks of flour, break up the white chocolate bar into small chunks and add to the bowl. Stir until just mixed, then spoon the mixture into the foil-lined pan.

7 ASK AN ADULT TO HELP YOU bake the brownies—they will take about 40 minutes in the center of the oven. To test if the brownies are ready, push a toothpick into the mixture about half way between the sides and the center. Pull out the toothpick—if it is clean, then the brownies are ready, if it is sticky, then cook for 5 minutes more.

8 Let the pan cool on a wire rack. When completely cold, remove the brownies from the pan, peel off the foil, then cut into 16 squares.

9 Store in an airtight container and eat within 5 days or freeze for up to 1 month.

warm fudge sauce

5 oz. bittersweet chocolate

2 tablespoons unsalted butter

3 tablespoons corn syrup

½ cup whole milk or half-and-half

SERVES 6

1 Break up the chocolate into chunks and put in a small saucepan. Add the butter, corn syrup, and milk or half-and-half. ASK AN ADULT TO HELP YOU put the pan on the lowest possible heat. When the butter and chocolate start to melt, stir gently every minute or so to make a smooth sauce. When the sauce is hot, ASK AN ADULT TO HELP YOU take the pan off the stove and pour the sauce carefully into a serving pitcher.

2 Serve the sauce with the brownies. If there is any leftover sauce, let it cool, then cover and store in the refrigerator ready for next time.

This is where lots of people start cooking—first mixing the batter, then graduating to beating egg whites (a rotary or electric hand mixer is a big help), folding the two together, then finally to cooking and flipping. The youngest child is usually "monitor" and is in charge of carrying each batch of just-cooked pancakes to the table.

1 To cook the pancakes, you will need a large, heavy skillet (nonstick or cast iron if possible), or a flat griddle, or electric skillet. If it isn't nonstick, rub the inside with a little oil.

2 ASK AN ADULT TO HELP YOU preheat the pan on the lowest setting while you make the batter. When you cook the pancakes, you should increase the heat up to medium-to-low.

3 To make the pancakes, put the flour, salt, and sugar in large bowl and mix well with a wire whisk. Make a hollow in the center of the flour.

4 Have another bowl ready for the egg whites. To separate the egg whites from the egg yolks, crack one of the eggs on the rim of the bowl so the shell is broken around the middle. Hold the egg over the empty bowl. Put both thumbs into this crack and gently pull the 2 halves of the shell away from each other so the clear egg white falls into the bowl and the round yellow yolk is left in one of the shells—this is not easy to do at first, so if the yolk falls into the bowl, lift it out with a spoon. Put the yolk into the hollow in the flour in the other bowl. Repeat with the other egg.

5 Pour the milk into the hollow in the flour on top of the yolks. Using the wire whisk, mix the milk and yolks together, then—a little at a time—stir in some of the flour. The liquid will become quite thick, and you may have to give it a good beat to get rid of the lumps.

6 To melt the butter, ASK AN ADULT TO HELP. Either put it in a small saucepan over the lowest possible heat, or put it in a microwave-proof dish and microwave on MEDIUM for about 20 seconds. Pour the melted butter into the batter and beat until you can't see it.

blueberry pancakes

a little oil, for greasing

¾ cup all-purpose flour

a big pinch of salt

1 tablespoon sugar

2 extra-large eggs

⅔ cup milk

2 tablespoons unsalted butter

6 oz. fresh or frozen blueberries

maple syrup, to serve

MAKES 12: SERVES 4

7 Using a rotary beater or electric hand mixer, beat the egg whites until they are very stiff and white—stiff enough not to fall out of the bowl if you turn it upside down (we test this over Grandpa's head—luckily he's bald).

8 Spoon the whites into the other bowl and gently stir the two mixtures with a large metal spoon. Try to use a "cut downwards and turn over" movement with the spoon instead of mixing round and round—this is called "folding." It is better to have small lumps of white than a completely smooth batter.

9 WITH AN ADULT TO HELP YOU, start cooking the pancakes. Turn up the heat under the pan to medium/low.

Add a large spoonful of batter to one side of the pan—it will spread out to about 4 inches across. Drop about 6 blueberries into the center of the pancake—it will still be liquid. After about 1 minute, check to see if small bubbles are breaking on the surface of the pancake and it has begun to set. Using a spatula, lift up the pancake just above the pan, then flip it back over into the pan to cook the other side. This may be messy to begin with, but they will always taste good. Cook the pancake for another minute, then lift out of the pan. Cook the rest of the mixture in the same way (try cooking 2 or 3 at once). Eat straight from the pan with any leftover blueberries and maple syrup.

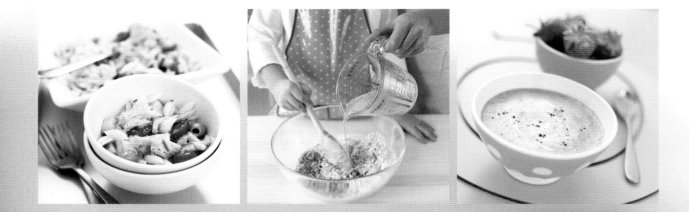

lunchboxes

Lunch doesn't need to be the same boring things day after day. Explain to your kids that they don't have to eat the same food as everyone else, and give them the chance to make themselves a special lunch. Start with sandwiches. Most people have cheese or ham, but show them the different kinds of bread on sale in bakeries and supermarkets. Have you tried a whole-wheat bagel or sourdough? If they usually go for cheese spread explore what else is on the cheese counter—Emmental has big holes and is quite mild, mozzarella is also mild and not just used in pizzas. If they like ham, try a mild salami or smoked turkey for a change (staff at the deli counter usually let you taste before you buy).

sandwiches

Everyone loves sandwiches, and we all have our favorite fillings. I've listed some of the lovely breads available, and just a few filling or spread ideas here. Mix and match them, or make up your own ideas.

Sliced bread and rolls Try making your own bread from the recipes in this book (pages 75 to 81), as well as buying interesting varieties from the supermarket bread counter, or from special bakers' stores. Our favorite filling is
• Tuna mayo—drain a 6 oz. can of tuna, then put the tuna in a small bowl. Stir in 2 tablespoons of mayonnaise and some ground black pepper. Cut a 2-inch piece of cucumber in half lengthwise, then cut both halves into very thin slices. Stir into the tuna. It can be kept in the refrigerator for 4 days. This mixture can also be used to fill tomatoes (cut off the tops then scrape out the seeds with a teaspoon) or the hollow in celery stalks.

Pita bread comes in white and whole wheat. Split them open at one end, then open out to make a pocket.
• Peel a carrot, cut off the ends, then grate the rest. Mix it with hummus (page 16) and fill (add some salad leaves too).
• Take 2 tablespoons of canned navy beans, drain, then mash with a fork, stir into guacamole (page 19), and fill the pita bread.
• Fill with baba ghanoush, then add thin slices of cucumber or lettuce leaf.

Bagels are sold white or whole wheat, plain or topped with seeds or onion flakes (there are also flavored bagels and sweet bagels). Slice in half carefully (take extra care if using a bagel slicer).
• Spread with cream cheese (plain or flavored with herbs) or cottage cheese. Add slices of tomato or smoked salmon, and cucumber.

Croissants can be large or small, plain or cheese-flavored. Carefully slice in half (they can fall apart), then fill. Because croissants are so buttery, they don't need spreading with butter.
• Fill with a slice of mild Swiss cheese and a slice of ham.
• Or a slice of cheese and some good strawberry jelly.

Wraps can also be large or small, made from wheat flour tortillas, plain or flavored, or from other flatbreads such as Indian village bread, or Egyptian lavash. Choose an easy-to-eat filling, such as sliced chicken or turkey with watercress or maybe guacamole. Spread the filling over the base, then roll it up tightly and wrap in plastic to hold it together in your lunchbox.

Small shell or "bow-tie" pasta works best. The dressing is a tangy lemon and olive oil, and you could use cooked corn instead of the olives.

tuna pasta salad

½ cup small pasta shapes

2 tablespoons pitted black or green olives or 2 tablespoons cooked corn

2-inch piece of cucumber

5 cherry tomatoes

6 oz. canned tuna

a few fresh chives

Olive oil dressing

2 tablespoons olive oil

1 tablespoon lemon juice

½ teaspoon Dijon or mild mustard

a pinch of salt

a pinch of freshly ground black pepper

MAKES ENOUGH FOR 2 MEALS

1 ASK AN ADULT TO HELP YOU cook the pasta. Fill a medium saucepan two-thirds full with cold water, then bring to a boil. Add a pinch of salt and the pasta, stir gently and let boil until tender— about 8 minutes (or follow the directions on the package).

2 Put a colander into the empty sink and ASK AN ADULT TO HELP YOU by straining the pasta into the colander. Rinse the pasta in the colander, under the cold tap, so it cools quickly and rinses off the starch. Drain thoroughly in the colander while you make the rest of the salad.

3 Put the olives in a bowl.

4 Cut the cucumber into about 6 thick slices, then cut each slice into quarters. Add to the bowl. Cut the tomatoes in half, and add.

5 Open the can of tuna with a can opener, then carefully drain off the liquid. The lid will be sharp, so remove it carefully. Tip the tuna into the bowl and break the lumps into small flakes with a fork. Using kitchen shears, snip the chives into small pieces and add to the bowl.

6 Put all the ingredients for the dressing into a screw-topped jar, and screw on the lid. Shake well, then open the jar and taste the dressing—you may want to add a little more salt or pepper.

7 Pour the dressing over the salad, then mix everything very gently with a metal spoon. Cover tightly and store in the refrigerator for up to 48 hours.

Another idea You can use ham or smoked turkey. Add to the other ingredients as for the tuna (above).

Couscous is a kind of pasta (not a grain) and it doesn't need cooking. You just add boiling water and let it soak for a little while. It makes a filling salad, but needs plenty of crunchy vegetables for color and texture.

couscous salad

¾ cup couscous

1 tablespoon olive oil

a big pinch of salt

a big pinch of dried herbes de Provence

2 scallions

1 medium carrot

6 cherry tomatoes

3 oz. sugar snap peas, green beans, or snowpeas

2 eggs

Dressing

2 tablespoons olive oil

1 tablespoon lemon juice

a big pinch of salt

a big pinch of freshly ground black pepper

SERVES 2

1 ASK AN ADULT TO HELP YOU to prepare the couscous. Bring water to a boil in a kettle. Put the couscous in a heatproof bowl, then add ¾ cup boiling water (or follow the instructions on the package). Add the oil, salt, and dried herbs, then gently stir with a spoon. Cover the bowl with a saucepan lid, tray, plate, or even a clean dish towel and leave for 5 minutes for the couscous to swell and soften.

2 Uncover the bowl, stir gently with a spoon, and let cool. While the couscous cools, prepare the rest of the salad.

3 First, use a small sharp knife to cut the scallions into thin rings.

4 Peel the carrot with a vegetable peeler, then cut off the ends with a small sharp knife. Make carrot ribbons with the vegetable peeler by peeling off long, thin lengths of carrot. Cut each tomato in half. Cut off the very ends of the sugar snap peas, green beans, or snowpeas.

5 ASK AND ADULT TO HELP YOU cook them—half fill a medium saucepan with cold water, bring to a boil over high heat, carefully add the vegetables, then cook for 3 minutes so they are still crunchy. Put a colander in the sink and ASK AN ADULT to strain the vegetables into the colander. Rinse under the cold tap to stop the vegetables cooking any more, then leave to drain really well.

6 To cook the eggs, put them in a small saucepan. Add cold water to the pan so the eggs are just covered. Put the pan over medium-low heat and set the timer for 12 minutes. ASK AN ADULT to remove the pan from the heat when the timer bell rings and put it into the sink. Turn on the cold tap and let it run over the eggs for 1 minute to cool them. Pour off the water, then gently tap the eggs on the work surface to crack the shells so you can peel them off. If small bits of shell stick to the eggs, rinse them under cold running water. Cut the eggs into quarters.

7 To make the dressing, put all the ingredients into a screw-top jar, put the lid on tightly, and shake well.

8 Add all the ingredients, including the dressing, to the cold couscous and gently mix the salad. Taste it, then add more salt, pepper, or lemon juice as needed. Cover the bowl tightly with plastic wrap and store in the refrigerator for up to 48 hours.

Other ideas
• Instead of the hard-cooked eggs, use cold cooked chicken (about 4 oz.) torn into shreds.
• Add a couple of tablespoons of toasted cashews.

These jam-filled cookies are sturdy enough to survive life in a lunchbox, and are fun to make. You can use raspberry or any other flavor jam. They will keep for a week in an airtight container.

gramma's raspberry buns

1 ASK AN ADULT TO HELP YOU preheat the oven to 400°F.

2 Rub the baking sheets with a little soft butter and a paper towel. This will prevent the buns from sticking to the baking sheets.

3 Put the flour and sugar in a bowl and mix well with your hand.

4 Cut the butter into tiny pieces with a round-bladed knife and add to the bowl.

5 Toss the pieces of butter in the flour so they are well coated, then start to rub the pieces of butter into the flour—to do this, pick up a handful of the mixture with your fingers, then rub the mixture between the very ends of your fingers so the bits of butter become smaller and smaller as they mix with the flour. Keep rubbing in until the whole mixture looks like crumbs.

6 Make a hollow in the center of the crumby mixture.

7 Break the egg into a small bowl, add the milk, and mix with a fork.

8 Tip the egg mixture into the hollow, then stir both mixtures together with a round-bladed knife to make a soft dough. If the dough is too dry and the crumbs won't stick together, add extra milk, 1 tablespoon at a time. If the dough is too wet and sticky, add 1 tablespoon extra flour until it is right.

9 Divide the dough into 16 even pieces. Roll each piece into a ball with your hands and set the balls well apart on the baking sheets.

10 Stick your finger in the middle of each ball to make a small hole (don't go right down to the bottom).

11 Using a teaspoon, put a pea-size amount of the jam in the hole, then pinch the dough back together to cover the hole (don't worry if it looks a bit messy at this point).

12 ASK AN ADULT TO HELP YOU bake the buns. Cook for 10 minutes at 400°F, then turn down the heat to 350°F and cook for 5 minutes more. Carefully remove the baking sheets from the oven, sprinkle the buns with a little sugar, and let cool for 5 minutes (the jam becomes incredibly hot in the oven and can easily burn you).

13 Using a spatula, transfer to a wire cooling rack and let cool completely.

1⅔ cups self-rising flour

scant ½ cup sugar, plus extra for sprinkling

1 stick unsalted butter from the refrigerator, plus extra for greasing the trays

1 extra-large egg

1 tablespoon milk

about 1 tablespoon raspberry jelly

2 baking sheets

MAKES 16

Rolled oats and crunchy seeds mixed with honey make a sweet end to lunch. Wrapped in foil, the oat bars stand up to life in a lunchbox, and the oats will give you energy all afternoon. If you are not keen on seeds, use raisins or chopped nuts instead—they're all good.

crunchy oat bars

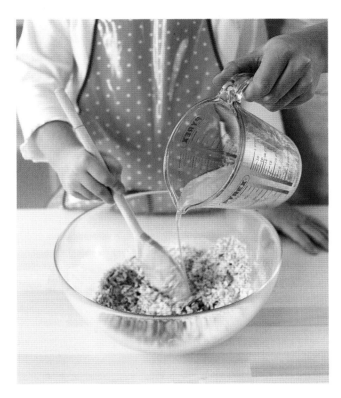

1 ASK AN ADULT TO HELP YOU preheat the oven to 400°F. While the oven is heating up, rub the baking pan with a little soft butter on a paper towel. This will prevent the bars sticking to the pan.

2 Measure the oats, flour, sugar, pumpkin seeds, sunflower seeds, and sesame seeds into a large bowl. Mix well with a wooden spoon.

3 Put the butter and honey into a small saucepan, and ASK AN ADULT to put it on the lowest heat on top of the stove until just melted.

4 Pour the melted butter and honey into the bowl with the oats and stir well.

5 Tip the oat mixture into the pan and spread it evenly with the wooden spoon. Lightly press it down so it all sticks together while it cooks.

6 ASK AN ADULT to put the pan in the oven and take it out after 20 minutes when it should look light golden brown. Stand the pan on a heatproof surface and, without touching the hot pan, gently cut the mixture into 9 squares (2 cuts each way).

7 Let cool then remove from the pan.

8 Store in an airtight container and eat within 1 week.

1 cup rolled oats

3 tablespoons self-rising flour

3 tablespoons sugar

1 tablespoon pumpkin seeds or raisins

1 tablespoon sunflower seeds or chopped nuts

1 tablespoon sesame seeds

7 tablespoons unsalted butter, plus extra for greasing the pan

1 tablespoon honey

a cake pan, 8 inches square

MAKES 9

Stevie fell in love with this heavenly soup one hot day at a Shaker restaurant in New England. It needs very ripe and juicy fruit. It is quick and easy to make in a blender and keeps well overnight in the refrigerator. Pour into a thermos, add an ice cube, then enjoy it after a long, hot morning in class.

cool strawberry soup

2 pints ripe strawberries

1 cup plain yogurt

1 tablespoon honey, or to taste

4 fresh mint or basil leaves

a pinch of salt and freshly ground black pepper

4 ice cubes

SERVES 4

1 Pinch out the green tops from the strawberries with your fingers or cut off the tops with a small knife. Put the fruit into a blender, then add the yogurt, honey, and herbs. Add a pinch of salt and about 3 grinds of the pepper mill.

2 ASK AN ADULT TO HELP YOU blend the mixture very briefly so the fruit becomes a thick, coarse purée rather than a smooth milkshake. Taste and add more honey, pepper, or salt if you like—the soup should not taste sweet.

3 If serving right away, stir in the ice cubes and serve in chilled bowls with a sprig of mint or basil on top.

4 If taking it to school, pour the mixture into individual thermos bottles, then add an ice cube to each one. Stir gently before eating.

5 The soup can also be stored in a pitcher, tightly covered, overnight in the refrigerator.

websites and mail order

King Arthur Flour Baker's Catalogue
P.O. Box 876
Norwich, Vermont 05055-0876
800-827-6836
www.kingarthurflour.com
A catalog of everything the home baker could ever need.

New York Cake & Baking Distributor
56 West 22nd Street
New York, NY 10010
800-942-2539 (outside NY)
212-675-2253
New York's most beloved baking ingredient and equipment retail store. Call for a catalog ($5 shipping cost).

Bridge Kitchenware
214 East 52nd Street
New York, NY 10022
800-274-3435 (outside NY)
212-688-4200
www.bridgekitchenware.com
Extensive selection of tart pans and baking equipment.

Broadway Panhandler
477 Broome Street
New York, NY 10013
212-966-3434
www.broadwaypanhandler.com
Extensive selection of tart pans and baking equipment.

Sur la Table
1765 6th Avenue South
Seattle, WA 98134
800-243-0852
www.surlatable.com
"Fine equipment for cooks and professional chefs."

Penzeys Spices
P.O. Box 933
Muskego, WI 53150
800-741-7787
www.penzeys.com
The source for all baking spices and extracts.

Chef's Catalog
111 Customer Way
Irving, TX 75039
800-884-2433
www.chefscatalog.com

Dean and Deluca
560 Broadway
New York NY 10012
800-221-7714
www.deandeluca.com

Zingerman's Mail Order
620 Phoenix Drive
Ann Arbor, MI 48108
888-636-8162
www.zingermans.com
Gourmet foods shop with a discriminating mail order service.

Williams-Sonoma
3250 Van Ness Avenue
San Francisco, CA 94109
877-812-6235
www.williamssonoma.com
Online and retail source for fine baking products and equipment.

conversion charts

Weights and measures have been rounded up or down slightly to make measuring easier.

volume equivalents:

american	metric	imperial
1 teaspoon	5 ml	
1 tablespoon	15 ml	
¼ cup	60 ml	2 fl.oz.
⅓ cup	75 ml	2½ fl.oz.
½ cup	125 ml	4 fl.oz.
⅔ cup	150 ml	5 fl.oz. (¼ pint)
¾ cup	175 ml	6 fl.oz.
1 cup	250 ml	8 fl.oz.

weight equivalents:

imperial	metric
1 oz.	25 g
2 oz.	50 g
3 oz.	75 g
4 oz.	125 g
5 oz.	150 g
6 oz.	175 g
7 oz.	200 g
8 oz. (½ lb.)	250 g
9 oz.	275 g
10 oz.	300 g
11 oz.	325 g
12 oz.	375 g
13 oz.	400 g
14 oz.	425 g
15 oz.	475 g
16 oz. (1 lb.)	500 g
2 1b.	1 kg

measurements:

inches	cm
¼ inch	5 mm
½ inch	1 cm
¾ inch	1.5 cm
1 inch	2.5 cm
2 inches	5 cm
3 inches	7 cm
4 inches	10 cm
5 inches	12 cm
6 inches	15 cm
7 inches	18 cm
8 inches	20 cm
9 inches	23 cm
10 inches	25 cm
11 inches	28 cm
12 inches	30 cm

oven temperatures:

225 °F	110 °C	Gas ¼
250 °F	120 °C	Gas ½
275 °F	140 °C	Gas 1
300 °F	150 °C	Gas 2
325 °F	160 °C	Gas 3
350 °F	180 °C	Gas 4
375 °F	190 °C	Gas 5
400 °F	200 °C	Gas 6
425 °F	220 °C	Gas 7
450 °F	230 °C	Gas 8
475 °F	240 °C	Gas 9

index

A

almonds: apple strudel, 106–7
amaretti cookies: apple strudel, 106–7
apples: apple strudel, 106–7
  juicy fruit crisp, 105
apricots: sweet and spicy soup, 57
avocados: flag salad, 39
  guacamole, 19

B

bagels, 114
baking, 58–81
bananas: chocolate bananas, 26
  fresh fruit brochettes, 98
  mango smoothie, 25
  strawberry milkshake, 25
bang bang chicken, 85
basil: cool strawberry soup, 124
  flag salad, 39
  fresh tomato summer sauce, 32
batter: pigs-in-blankets, 51
beef rendang, 93
best-ever chocolate cake, 64
biscuits: cheese and chilli biscuits, 72
  lemon and thyme biscuits, 70–1
blackberries: juicy fruit crisp, 105
blueberries: blueberry pancakes, 110–11
  apple strudel, 106–7
  cinnamon meringues with fresh fruit, 102
  juicy fruit crisp, 105
bread, 75–7
  braided loaf, 76
  cheese bread, 76
  cheese melts, 15
  cinnamon toast, 10
  Cornish bread, 78
  Grant loaf, 81
  grilled cheese sandwich, 13
  pita bread, 114
  rolls, 76
  sandwiches, 114
  shiny bread, 76

brochettes, fresh fruit, 98
brownies and ice cream, 109
buns, Gramma's raspberry, 120
buttermilk: pizza dough, 40

C

cakes: best-ever chocolate cake, 64
  brownies, 109
  lemon drizzle loaf cake, 66
  toffee loaf cake, 69
cannellini beans: sandwich filling, 114
cardamom pods: beef rendang, 93
carrots: bang bang chicken, 85
  couscous salad, 119
  roasties, 94
cheese: cheese and chile biscuits, 72
  cheese bread, 76
  cheese melts, 15
  croissants, 114
  flag salad, 39
  grilled cheese sandwich, 13
  pea and Parmesan risotto, 43
  pizza, 40–1
chicken: bang bang chicken, 85
  Italian roast chicken, 87
  Thai meatballs with chicken, 88
chickpeas: hummus, 16
chile sauce: Thai meatballs with chicken, 88
chipolata sausages: pigs-in-blankets, 51
chips, home-baked tortilla, 19
chives: pink dolly's pasta, 36
  fresh tomato sauce with pasta, 32
chocolate: best-ever chocolate cake, 64
  brownies and ice cream, 109
  chocolate bananas, 26
  double chocolate muffins, 63
  real hot chocolate, 22
  warm fudge sauce, 109
cilantro: Thai meatballs with chicken, 88
cinnamon: apple strudel, 106–7
  cinnamon meringues with fresh fruit, 102
  cinnamon toast, 10
cookies: Gramma's raspberry buns, 120
cool strawberry soup, 124

corn: corn-on-the-cob, 96
  Spanish omelet, 52
  tuna pasta salad, 116
Cornish bread, 78
cottage cheese: sandwich filling, 114
couscous salad, 119
cream cheese: sandwich filling, 114
croissants, 114
crunchy oat bars, 123
cucumber: bang bang chicken, 85
  cucumber sushi rolls, 46, 49
  tuna mayo, 114
  tuna pasta salad, 116
curries: beef rendang, 93

D

desserts, 98–111
  blueberry pancakes, 110–11
  brownies and ice cream, 109
  apple strudel, 106–7
  cinnamon meringues with fresh fruit, 102
  fresh fruit brochettes, 98
  juicy fruit crisp, 105
  little strawberry tarts, 101
dips: guacamole, 19
  hummus, 16
dolly's pasta, 36
double chocolate muffins, 63
dough: bread, 75–7
  pizza, 40
dressings: herb, 44
  olive oil, 116
dried fruit: Cornish bread, 78
drinks: fresh raspberry lemonade, 20
  mango smoothie, 25
  real hot chocolate, 22
  strawberry milkshake, 25

E

egg cup sushi, 47–9
eggs: couscous salad, 119
  meringues, 102
  Spanish omelet, 52
endive "boats," smoked salmon in, 44

F

fettuccine: dolly's pasta, 36
flag salad, 39
fresh fruit brochettes, 98
fresh peach salsa, 15

fresh raspberry lemonade, 20
fresh tomato sauce with pasta, 32
fruit: cinnamon meringues with fresh fruit, 102
  fresh fruit brochettes, 98
  see also individual types of fruit
fruit juice:frozen treats, 28
fudge sauce, 109

G

garlic: beef rendang, 93
  Italian roast chicken, 87
ginger: beef rendang, 93
  gingerbread people, 60
  salmon phyllo parcels, 90
Gramma's raspberry buns, 120
Grant loaf, 81
green beans: couscous salad, 119
grilled cheese sandwich, 13
guacamole, 19
  sandwich filling, 114

H

herb dressing, 44
home-baked tortilla chips, 19
honey: cool strawberry soup, 124
hot red pepper flakes: cheese and chile biscuits, 72
hummus, 16
  sandwich filling, 114

I

ice cream: brownies and ice cream, 109
  cinnamon meringues with fresh fruit, 102
Italian roast chicken, 87

J

jam: Gramma's raspberry buns, 120
juicy fruit crisp, 105

K

kiwi: fresh fruit brochettes, 98

L

lemons: fresh raspberry lemonade, 20
  Italian roast chicken, 87
  lemon and thyme biscuits, 70–1

lemon drizzle loaf cake, 66
zingy pasta, 35
lentils: sweet and spicy soup, 57
tomato and red lentil soup, 54
lettuce: flag salad, 39
smoked salmon in endive
"boats," 44
little strawberry tarts, 101
lunchboxes, 112–25

M
mango smoothie, 25
mayo, tuna, 114
meatballs, Thai, 88
meringues: cinnamon meringues
with fresh fruit, 102
milk: lemon and thyme scones,
70–1
real hot chocolate, 22
strawberry milkshake, 25
warm fudge sauce, 109
mint: cool strawberry soup, 124
muffins, double chocolate, 63

N
nectarines: fresh fruit brochettes, 98
nori seaweed: sushi, 46
nuts: chocolate bananas, 26
crunchy oat bars, 123
toffee loaf cake, 69

O
oats: crunchy oat bars, 123
olive oil dressing, 116
olives: tuna pasta salad, 116
omelet, Spanish, 52
onions: beef rendang, 93
orange juice: mango smoothie, 25

P
pancakes: blueberry pancakes,
110–11
parsley: hummus, 16
parsnips: roasties, 94
pasta: dolly's pasta, 36
fresh tomato summer sauce,
32
tuna pasta salad, 116
zingy pasta, 35
pastries: apple strudel, 106–7
little strawberry tarts, 101
salmon phyllo packages, 90
peaches: fresh fruit brochettes, 98
fresh peach salsa, 15
juicy fruit crisp, 105

peanut butter: bang bang
chicken, 85
pears: juicy fruit crisp, 105
peas: pea and Parmesan risotto, 43
Spanish omelet, 52
pecans: toffee loaf cake, 69
peppers: Spanish omelet, 52
phyllo pastry: apple strudel,
106–7
salmon phyllo packages,
90
pigs-in-blankets, 51
pita bread, 114
pizza, 40–1
bread bases, 76
potatoes: Armenian soup, 57
roasties, 94
Spanish omelet, 52
pumpkin seeds: crunchy oat bars,
123

R
raisins: apple strudel, 106–7
crunchy oat bars, 123
raspberries: cinnamon meringues
with fresh fruit, 102
fresh raspberry lemonade, 20
juicy fruit crisp, 105
raspberry jam: Gramma's
raspberry buns, 120
real hot chocolate, 22
red currant jelly: little strawberry
tarts, 101
rice: pea and Parmesan risotto, 43
Thai fragrant rice, 89
two kinds of sushi, 46–9
rice vinegar: sushi, 46
risotto, pea and Parmesan, 43
roasties, 94
rolls, 76, 114
rosemary: Italian roast chicken, 87
roasties, 94

S
saffron: Cornish bread, 78
salads: bang bang chicken, 85
couscous salad, 119
flag salad, 39
tuna pasta salad, 116
salmon: salmon phyllo packages,
90
see also smoked salmon
salsa, fresh peach, 15
sandwiches, 114
grilled cheese sandwich, 13

sauces: fresh tomato sauce with
pasta, 32
warm fudge sauce, 109
sausages: pigs-in-blankets, 51
scallions: Spanish omelet, 52
seaweed: sushi, 46
sesame seeds: crunchy oat
flapjacks, 123
shiny bread, 76
smoked mackerel: pasta salad, 116
smoked salmon: dolly's pasta, 36
smoked salmon in endive
"boats," 44
sushi, 46
smoked trout: dolly's pasta, 36
pasta salad, 116
smoked trout in endive "boats,"
44
smoothie, mango, 25
snacks, 8–29
snowpeas: couscous salad, 119
soups: sweet and spicy soup, 57
cool strawberry soup, 124
tomato and red lentil soup, 54
sour cream: best-ever chocolate
cake, 64
spaghetti: fresh tomato sauce
with pasta, 32
Spanish omelet, 52
strawberries: cinnamon meringues
with fresh fruit, 102
cool strawberry soup, 124
fresh fruit brochettes, 98
little strawberry tarts, 101
strawberry milkshake, 25
strudel, apple, 106–7
sugar snap peas: couscous salad,
119
sunflower seeds: crunchy oat
bars, 123
suppers, 30–57
sushi, 46–9
sweet and spicy soup, 57
sweet potatoes: roasties, 94

T
tagliolini: zingy pasta, 35
tahini paste: hummus, 16
tamarind purée: beef rendang, 93
tarts, little strawberry, 101
Thai fragrant rice, 89
Thai meatballs with chicken, 88
thyme: Italian roast chicken, 87
lemon and thyme biscuits,
70–1

roasties, 94
toast: cheese melts, 15
cinnamon toast, 10
grilled cheese sandwich, 13
toffee loaf cake, 69
tomatoes: couscous salad, 119
flag salad, 39
fresh peach salsa, 15
fresh tomato sauce with pasta,
32
guacamole, 19
pizza, 40–1
Spanish omelet, 52
tomato and red lentil soup, 54
tuna pasta salad, 116
tortillas: home-baked tortilla
chips, 19
wraps, 114
trout see smoked trout
tuna: tuna mayo, 114
tuna pasta salad, 116
turkey, Thai meatballs with, 88
two kinds of sushi, 46–9

V
vegetables: roasties, 94
Spanish omelet, 52
see also individual types of
vegetables
vinegar: sushi, 46–7

W
warm fudge sauce, 109
watercress: flag salad, 39
zingy pasta, 35
wraps, 114

Y
yeast, 75–7
yogurt: cool strawberry soup, 124
frozen treats, 28
pizza dough, 40
toffee loaf cake, 69

Z
zingy pasta, 35